Changing the NFD

Additional books by author:

Firehouse Fraternity Oral History Series:
Volume I: Becoming a Firefighter
Volume II: Life Between Alarms
Volume III: Equipment
Volume IV: Responding
Volume V: Riots to Renaissance

The Newark Riots: A View from the Firehouse

An Eerie Silence: An Oral History of Newark
Firefighters at the WTC

Hervey's Boys: New Jersey's First Chinese Community
1870-1886 (And What Happened After That)

Fiction:
The Firebox Stalker
The Hand Life Dealt you
A-zou: A Woman Living in Interesting Times

Children's Fiction:
A Hundred Battles (YA)
A Broken Glass (YA)
Balancing Act (Middle Grade)

The Firehouse Fraternity

An Oral History of the
Newark Fire Department

Volume VI

Changing the NFD

Neal Stoffers

Springfield and Hunterdon Publishing
Copyright 2011
www.newarkfireoralhistory.com

First Printing: 2011

ISBN: 978-1-970034-15-8

Springfield and Hunterdon Publishing
East Brunswick, NJ 08816-5852

Dedicated to past, present, and future generations of Newark firefighters, and especially to the 67 firefighters who made the ultimate sacrifice upholding their oath to protect the lives and property of Newark's citizens.

Contents

Acknowledgements

The credit for much of this book goes to the members of the Newark Fire Department who gave so generously of their time to take part in my oral history project. The hours of recorded conversations they contributed will help preserve the history of Newark's fire department and of Newark itself. A list of those interviewed appears at the end of the book. This is their story. I am honored to tell it.

Foreword

This book is the last of a series which recounts the experiences of Newark firefighters. Beginning with the memories of a firefighter appointed in 1942, the series tells the story of New Jersey's largest city and her fire department as seen through the eyes of the men manning her firehouses. I have attempted to group related subjects together to give the reader a true feel for various aspects of the fire service. The comments of the men I interviewed are presented in order of appointment date. This method is an attempt to give a better picture of the chronology of the dramatic changes which occurred in the city of Newark and the fire service in general.

The seeds of these books were unknowingly planted in a small firehouse on Springfield Avenue and Hunterdon Street. It was here as a young firefighter that I sat in the kitchen of Six Engine and listened to conversations between veteran firefighters, Captains, and Deputy Chiefs about a city and fire department that existed in another time.

In June of 1991, I began an oral history project to preserve the memories of these men and the generations of firefighters who followed. The purpose of this project was to capture not only the words, but the texture of their experiences. What was a firefighting career like during this period in Newark and by extrapolation in America? Fire departments across the country have shared the experiences of the NFD in one way or another. Whether read by a professional firefighter from New York City or by a volunteer firefighter from a small rural community, the stories will be familiar. The fire service is a small world with a common purpose.

It is hoped that what is recorded here will show both a bygone era and the evolution of the Newark Fire Department into its present form. If others outside the fire service walk away with a better understanding of the firefighters and the fire departments that protect them, my time over the past years will have been well spent.

On a final note, this series of books was written over the course of the past five years. Beginning with the first interview, the oral history project that led to the books spanned two decades. Approximately half of the interviews I conducted for this project are included. The other half and any additional interviews need to be transcribed, indexed, organized, and edited before another book can be printed. I would like to bring the oral history forward to the present (the last entrance exam recounted in the present series of books was taken in 1977), but do not anticipate publishing anything more for a number of years if ever (life can be capricious). It has been an honor (and a lot of fun) to gather the stories and then visit firehouses, attend union picnics and Christmas parties with these books. I hope the readers have enjoyed the books and the memories they preserve as much as I enjoyed the company of Newark's bravest over the last 34 years.

Chapter One: Labor Union

Redden: When I started, the FMBA* represented everybody on the job. Of course the FMBA was like a company union. They more or less got what was offered to them. They were a social organization, a political organization. If you got promoted to captain and you were in with the FMBA, you could say, "Hey, I want to go here. I want to go there." And you'd go there, but I didn't know anybody in the FMBA, so I took what was left.

They didn't exactly negotiate pay raises. I don't think there were any negotiations going on. Essentially, what would happen is they would go see the Commissioner or Director, whatever they called him, and say, "Look, we would like to have this much." He would say, "Well, I'm going to give you this much." That's it. I don't think we got any benefits until they got into the regular union. Then you start getting clothing allowance, personal days, and so forth.

I guess when I was a Battalion Chief or getting to be a Deputy Chief, the firemen were FMBA, then they were Teamsters, and then they were AFL-CIO. The officers became affiliated with the AFL-CIO. That was a different situation. The bargaining unit was stronger because it wasn't a company union. They were able people, who negotiated pay raises, negotiated benefits and so forth. So, it was a much stronger situation than the FMBA.

Kinnear: In those days we really didn't have a union to fight. There was the FMBA which had no power, no arbitration power, so we were at the mercy of the politicians. If they wanted to give you a raise this year they did. If they didn't, they didn't. Election year they always gave you a raise. I don't

* Firemen's Mutual Benevolent Association

remember when the unions first came in. It was a good thing for the fire department at that time. Maybe now they've gotten a little too strong, but at that time it was a good thing because you could negotiate, arbitrate, and things like that. But I remember we usually didn't get raises before the union. They just didn't give you a raise and that was it. The raises sometimes were three or four hundred, five hundred dollars a year.

The FMBA was a social club. A social union, I would call it. You paid dues. You paid good and welfare, but it had no power. No real power like the union has today. They'd sit down with the politicians; ask for things. Sometimes they got them, sometimes they didn't. If the politicians said no, that was it. You just didn't get.

F. Grehl: The FMBA was basically a social and political club. There were certain things they could do to ease tensions among the people out there for the politicians. The politicians in turn would give them their requests for transfers for different people. That gave them like an upper hand over the membership because they could get you a transfer, get you transferred, or something of that nature. It was a clique. Those who were in were in solid. Those who were out, got all the blacks in their firehouses when they came on. It wasn't until around the early '70s, maybe even earlier than that, when the unions really started to form.

The FMBA was the most powerful one because they had a state organization. Through the various locals they would go to the state organization to enact the fifty-six hour work week, to enact the forty-two hour work week, to enact the residency rule. That's where we worked, through the state organization to get those things done. It wasn't until they got the arbitration law passed, that the unions became very, very powerful.

Up until that point, it was up to the politicians to decide what they were going to give you.

Years ago, every election year you'd get hit for a twenty dollar, thirty dollar contribution and you would get back a two, three hundred dollar pay raise. You'd pay ten percent in order to get a raise, but they were covered by contributions to a picnic or tickets, things like that. Of course, today it's almost that you have to have tickets. There's no other way of getting around except through buying tickets. You have to do it a little differently.

Masterson: At the very beginning it was a thirty dollar collection. That was like taking the baby's milk money. That was a lot of money then, thirty dollars. They had the five commissioners at that time. I don't know who got it or if they divided it, but we got the first five hundred dollars for that. Some guys wouldn't come up with it. They were blackballed. One time we wanted a five hundred dollar raise and we were out on a referendum. They actually used the city money to campaign against this in the paper. They put ads that said we can't afford to pay them the money. They knocked us out. Then Hughie Addonizio came along. Without us even asking he gave us a thousand dollar raise. We thought this guy walked on water.

After they went on strike that time, the state passed binding arbitration. When that came in it was the best thing. Because now we knew eventually we were going to get it. But up until then we were at their mercy. Up until then you always had to come up with something. Pay politicians who were as crooked as a cast iron cork screw.

Wall: As a Battalion Chief, they changed the state law on labor negotiations and you almost had to become a union to negotiate. We were at that time the Fire Officers Association which was set up on the Masonic theory. They changed the president every year. You could go in as the Sergeant at Arms. You went up the rank; you were the president; and you were out. So, they would elect a real nice guy for Sergeant at Arms, but he's the most incompetent son of a gun in the world by the time he became the president. Jimmy Marinucci and myself and maybe Freddy Grehl said, "Why don't we organize a union?" They said, "Well, you're the most articulate of the bunch of us. Why don't you lead it off?" I said, "Okay." So I went to Redden. I said, "It's a slow summer, Chief. We Battalion Chiefs have decided we're going to organize an officers union." He said, "Ah, for Christ's sake." "No, Joe, you'd be better off. You'd be dealing with a real union." So that's how we got involved with the firefighters. We organized it and overwhelmingly we won the election when the election came up. I was president about eight years. When I made Deputy Chief, I was still president.

McGee: To be perfectly honest, raises were basically gotten through contributions. That's the way it was in the older days. But that didn't work out and it shouldn't have worked out. We really took a shellacking for most of the negotiations. Because it was the kind of union where the city could say this is the way it's going to be and that was it.

Binding arbitration was the thing, if you want to pick one particular change in policy that caused the city to lose complete control over you. They had to give. It had to be a fair thing. We would present a proposal and the city would present a proposal and the arbitrator would rule. And it was binding on both parties. Before, we were at the mercy of the city. That's where the fire department started to make some great strides in terms of salary, benefits, and so forth. I don't know who that was due to. Definitely the union presidents and guys who stuck their necks out, because if we were at the city's mercy, believe me you'd still be in trouble. Any city, that's their job.

Stoffers: Back when I think Carlin was the mayor, they wouldn't pay you overtime. They'd give you time back. There were so many hours. Some guys got over a hundred and sixty hours storm time just in one period. Then Addonizzio got elected the following May. They kept pushing and pushing and pushing. They finally decided they never would be able to give all the time back. So, they settled and I think they paid everybody for forty two hours; wiped everything off the books. That's when we started pushing for a stronger union.

McGrory: The unions got an awful lot for us. They had to get a little here, a little chip away there. The city is looking for givebacks now, but the unions worked for all this. The union in the old time would be called a company union. Because it didn't have that much power, it wasn't affiliated with a national union or anything. Before they got binding arbitration, the only way to get a raise was to pay for it.

Charpentier: Until we got a union contract, the FMBA was a social thing. You paid dues, but it was like a social thing. They had no clout. Even if a guy didn't belong to the FMBA and he knew somebody who knew somebody, he got what he wanted. Where a guy, who really was in a busy company for fifteen, twenty years, was getting a little older, who would have liked to put the remaining few years in a little slower company, he might have been overlooked for somebody who just came on the job who knew somebody and he got what he wanted.

The role of the FMBA changed with the arbitration laws to an extent. They had a little power. I wouldn't say to the way a union should have been, but to a point I think they did have some say into what was going on. Carragher: There was no union. There was no union, no benefits or anything when I went on the job. We had no medical, no dental or anything. The city did with you what they wanted. I think in 1960 they had an election for mayor. Leo Carlin was running for re-election. It was the day before election we got Blue Cross/Blue Shield and Prudential. The day before election, he gave it to us. Then negotiations were just the firemen's union president, Nick Dominico at the time, got together with the mayor. They talked things over. This is what we're giving you. It wasn't what you wanted. It was what they were going to give you.

Now another point, that first year on the job, 1960, when I was in Nine Engine, in December we had two major snowstorms. Both were around twenty or twenty- two inches of snow. Then I worked two hundred hours on recall in December of that first year on the job. We had two hundred hours of recall. No pay, nothing, they just told you to stay. We had the three shifts on duty at one time in the firehouse. Nine Engine was a two-piece company. With the two-piece company we could man two apparatus. Some of the guys went out and shoveled snow and the two apparatus could ride as two different companies. The first piece would go out to this fire and the second piece would pull up and be in service as Nine Engine, so Nine wouldn't go out of service. It would be there. That's how they worked it then. If you had the right chief, he would give you back the time.

We probably got the union around '70. The FMBA started getting more advanced there. I don't think we really had benefits per se until then. What makes me think this is we had the twelve holidays per year that Caufield gave us in 1965. With the Trubahorn court decision we got sixty-five days which runs out to about five and a half years. That would bring you into '70. So, actually the first firemen's contract was probably in '70 and that's when you had a union. That's when they did away with the twelve days on the books and gave you twelve paid holidays. So, I would think you had a union somewhere around '70. Now they did have a professional officers' union that I did belong to in 1965, but it wasn't for bargaining. It was like an officers' association, but you didn't have bargaining rights. They gave you what they wanted. That's what we should say. You got bargaining rights probably around 1970.*

Haran: The union used to control all the transfers when we had the FMBA. That was a benevolent association. They were the ones who negotiated our raise. You had to go down and kiss the ring for a transfer and everything else. When I came on the job and I had just bought all my equipment; I was making eighty dollars a week. A guy came up to me and says to me, "You have your forty dollar assessment?" Forty dollars was half a week's pay. I make eighteen hundred dollars a week now. That's like a guy coming up to me and asking me for nine hundred dollars today. Do you think I should balk at that? Absolutely, nine hundred dollars is serious money. That's what forty dollars was back then, half a week's pay. I said, "Assessment? For what?" He said, "We're getting up a dough bag. We're going for a raise." That's what they used to do. They used to give Hughie Addonizio or Mayor Carlin X amount of money. They used to get half that money and then certain councilmen we want in got the rest of it. That's what we were told. But there were dough bags and they had done that for years. And that's how we used to get our raises. We were at their mercy. Now we

---

* The state allowed representation elections for public workers in 1968. (Star Ledger February 5, 2003)

7

could have given him all that money and he could have told us, "Go pound salt."

I remember years ago, we got into a coalition with the Newark Police Department because we always had parity. We had a big meeting up at Ferrara's hall on Verona Avenue and Broadway. That was a big meeting with the cops and firemen. We were going to pass out literature. The cops backed out of it. They didn't want anything to do with it. The firemen continued on with it. This literature had kids with faces burned and burned bodies and fires. They put firemen out on McCarter Highway and all the main streets coming in off of Route One. We were out there in the morning rush hour and in the evening rush hour passing out adverse literature. This could happen. I didn't want to do that kind of stuff. But that's the kind of stuff we used to have to do for a raise back then, to go from eight thousand to ten thousand or ten thousand five. We had to kiss ass to get a raise.

Then finally we got binding arbitration, which was a big thing for us. We got this and we got that. It was always, you never give up anything. You don't give up anything you've got. When I came on the job we got no holidays, you didn't get any holidays. That's why I'm getting the Trubahorn days now. I'm getting sixty-five of them because I was on the job at the beginning. Now that was the kind of stuff they pulled back then. We were awarded thirteen paid holidays and they didn't pay us for five years. They said they can't. This guy Trubahron took them to court and won it. Now they said, "Well, we can't pay you, so what we'll do is we'll give you the money when you retire." That's how it came about, but five years they stalled us off on holiday pay.

We never got personal days. Now we get three personal days. What else did we get? When I came on the job we didn't get all these vacation days. We didn't get medicals when I first came on. We got it shortly thereafter.

Butler: Well, prior to binding arbitration the union wasn't totally powerless. The old days (and they can be talked about now because just about everybody involved is gone), the old days were the dough bag days. The FMBA had a collector in each house. Single, double, triple house one guy was the dues collector because there was no dues check off on the payroll. You paid your monthly dues and assessments to this collector. You had a little receipt book which would last you maybe five or ten years and each month you paid, he'd sign it. He'd have all the money, make the trip to the union office, and that was our money. You had yearly dough bags to be given to buy tickets for politicians' affairs. I remember many dough bag years it was fifty bucks a head collected for eight hundred, a thousand guys. That gave you a lot of money and you were able to make impressions upon the politicians to favor you with contracts. Then binding arbitration came in and really cut just about all of that out.

Some of the politicians then would just keep approaching you. "Well, you used to buy tickets, why don't you buy tickets anymore?" Basically the mayor is the only one who we really can support through political donations and feel that he can do something for us. From time to time some of the councilmen can if something comes up in front of them relating to the fire department, the police department, but the mayor's the one because he'll tell the BA or whoever is negotiating the contract, "Well, go this far with them. Let them have this and that." At other times if you don't kick in, he'd say, "No don't give them anything. Stay your position at three percent, whatever it is, and that's the end of it." The mayor can get to the guy and tell him soften up a little bit. Give the extra one percent or give them the extra holiday, whatever they want." That can be done. You could never say for sure, positively, that I know exactly for x number of tickets something was done, but the theory is there. That's the way it operated.

Langenbach: When I first came on the job there was no binding arbitration, there was no arbitration at all. It was you went with your hat in your hand to the mayor and asked for a raise and if they said yes you got one and if they said no you didn't. That was the big thing. We had three days personal days. They were part of the contract. I don't know where they came from. You didn't have to kiss any rings. We were represented by the Teamsters. Then we went on our own for a while. When Bobby Dougherty was president, we were on our own. Then we went back to the FMBA, then to the IAFF*. Now they're back on their own again and the officers went to the IAFF.

The union made a lot of things better on the job. Money wise of course. I know a couple of contracts ago they started talking about taking care of the retired guys, which (as a retired guy) I really appreciate and our benefits got better. They made significant changes in the job. Do I agree with everything they did? Absolutely not, some changes were good and some not so good. The job's getting made safer or is it? I don't know. But thanks to an aggressive stance by the unions, everybody just got together and said enough is enough. We'll see how it all pans out.

T. Grehl: Binding arbitration was a great thing, because it took the strike away. It eliminated that. It eliminated the slicing of tires between the ranks and the officers and firemen. Who got mad at whom because you couldn't go on strike? That was their way of saying "You can't go on strike, but

---

* International Association of Firefighters

we're going to give you another avenue." Whoever is better prepared and proves better wins. I think that's fair.

The officer's union right now is trying to bring it to the super professional level. They're doing a lot of real positive things as far as really stepping it up to be professional. If the ruling that an officer must replace an officer when someone is on vacation or sick is not overturned in the courts and it stays that way, I see our department as making tremendous strides and going upward.

Gesualdo: When I first came on, Tony Nardone was president. I don't seem to remember there being as much friction between the city and the union, nothing that was ever really discussed at any length in the firehouse. The change seemed to come later on. As far as the negotiations, they seemed to run over the end of the contract, always got a retroactive check. Issues were personal days, vacation days; things like that. There's really not much you can contest with the fire department. You do just about whatever they ask you to do. The people call you for everything and then we handle everything. So, most of the sticking points were with personal days off, vacation days, and pay.

Not having been too involved with the union at the time, I'm really not sure how they negotiated, but I know most of the time it went into arbitration. Initially the union would send out forms to all the firehouses. They asked the guys, the firefighters, what they thought were the most important issues to push for. Whether they used that or not as a guideline or took that for what it was worth, I'm not sure. But they sent them out. We filled them out, pay increase, hospitalization, that type of thing. Then I always remember it going into arbitration and coming out usually with half of what we asked for. Seven, eight percent, you'd get four, four and a half at the time, maybe five. I remember a couple of five percent increases, but it always seemed to work out. It sometimes took up to a year. I guess that was probably the longest I can remember. But that was considered as being normal. It just seemed to be the way things went.

I can remember there being a hospitalization plan. Personal days, I think have been the same for the last twenty-six years: three days. Vacations increased. The hospitalization I know. I had a wife and children at the time, two children when I came on. I remember that being a big issue with me, so it was probably a pretty decent plan because I didn't have to go out and get any extra protection. It seemed to be adequate.

Chapter Two: Strike

Redden: Okay, the firemen's strike, the city was fighting with the State about getting money. And to this day I think the politicians kind of talked the fire department into going on strike to let the State know how bad things were. So, it was a twenty-four hour strike. We recalled all the officers.

I think it's the worst thing that ever happened to the fire department quite frankly. There were a lot of enmities between the firemen and the officers. There was damage done to cars, some of the officers' cars parked around the firehouses. I know it happened up at Six Engine. It lasted twenty-four hours and they came back. That was the extent of it. There was nothing done to the firemen for striking. Again I think the politicians enjoyed the situation because it highlighted the problem. I may be wrong, but that's what I think.

Kinnear: The firemen went on strike. I was an officer at the time, so I wasn't involved except working. The state had promised to give us the money to give the firemen a twenty-five hundred dollar raise. The officers were going to get more because it was a percentage increase. If the firemen were getting twenty-five hundred, the captains were going to get three thousand. Battalion Chiefs were going to get thirty-five hundred. The officers were getting what they wanted and now the firemen said, "Well, wait a minute. If he's getting three thousand and I'm only getting twenty-five hundred, that's not right." That's how I recall what happened. The officers shouldn't get a percentage. They should get the same amount as the firemen.

I sympathized with the guys. I was with a couple of them at five o'clock at night and they were still debating whether to go in. I said, "Well, I have to go in, because we're not going on strike." They finally decided not to go in.

There were some incidents. There was an incident at Two Engine. A fireman who was supposedly on strike was hanging around and he was told to leave. I think they got annoyed. I guess there was some resentment, but it didn't last long. I never saw any resentment. I think guys knew how I felt. I felt the percentages were right. I felt they did have some sort of grievance, but I didn't think they had enough of a grievance to go on strike. But they had to do what they had to do and they did it. If there was resentment, it didn't last long.

Masters: Strike? Yes, now that you remind me, we did go on strike. Just a few guys that went in, but I stayed out. The firehouses were manned by skeleton crews. If there was a working fire, they couldn't do a thing. But what did it accomplish? Nothing.

F. Grehl: The strike brought on arbitration because of the fact that they left the city so destitute. The state organization managed, through the legislators, to get arbitration laws passed which forbid them to strike. But it gave them the right to binding arbitration. Before then you had no way. You would say, "Hey you gave me a two hundred dollar raise. The cost of living went way sky high. It was nowhere near right. Why don't you do what's right?"

They called a strike this one night to try to emphasize their demands and it got a little bit out of hand with some of the fellows who were over active. Officers were called upon to do just about anything. Chief JanTausch was tillering Nine Truck. I think Brennan was down in Five Truck driving Five Truck. All the officers were out doing something. I was a Battalion Chief at the time and was assigned to the South Ward. They gave me a gig and said, "Go out and handle the South Ward. Try and keep things under control out there."

I had a young fellow named Bill Weber. He's a captain now. He was a brand new probationary fireman. He was only on about a month when this thing took effect. I had a pretty good rapport with people. I was tipped off that they were going to strike that night and also tipped off through the Officers' Association that the officers were all expected to stay on duty. So I went up to Seventeen Engine, got them all together, and said, "You fellows do what you think you have to do, but there'll be a tremendous amount of animosity toward anyone who doesn't go out on strike with the others. There's one thing I want you to think of and that's Bill. Bill's a probationary fireman, one month on the job. He's a probationary fireman for one year during which they could fire him without having a hearing. You force him to go on strike they could fire him if this thing gets out of hand. Do you want that to happen?" So, they left him alone. They let him and a few other probationary firemen work.

Most of the guys on strike were reasonable. They didn't cause any trouble, except one group that was running around vandalizing. They cut our tires. My car was in Six Engine's driveway, Brennan's car was there and Nolen's car. They sliced our tires on us. I went to the FMBA. I said, "Hey, now you have to pay for my tires. Your guys did it so you have to pay for it." "We don't know who did it." Of course when the investigation came, everything was slid over, cleared up. Actually, it was probably the best thing. If they had gone through it, who did what and prosecuted them, it would only have carried the thing on longer. Probably turned out best, but I still had to buy new tires.

Vesey: They had a one-day strike. If you were on duty when they walked, you were more or less trapped in the house because everybody was on strike. They didn't show up. They almost got a hundred per cent turn out to strike. Like I said, it didn't last that long. There was a little bitterness after a while, but we finally got the raise. We wound up with about five percent. You picked up another couple of hundred bucks. You had to do it.

Deutch: I did feel bad about the strike. Nobody ever thought we would strike the city. We actually were very fortunate because the first tour didn't have to think about it until half way through the day it was settled. We stood outside of the firehouse and the captain said, "You coming in or aren't you coming in?" The union was telling us don't go in. The captain was saying, "It's up to you. It's up to you. If you think you're doing the right thing or you don't think you're doing the right thing." Well, probably half an hour we stood out; then we went in. We didn't want to break the strike. We didn't want to hurt the city either. That was a very touchy time. I think there were a couple of men who worked. The rest thought about it for a while. It was settled by the time we were due our first day in.

Wall: I think the firefighter's strike was probably one of the most destructive things that happened to the Newark Fire Department. I saw a definite change in attitudes towards people. I think it was more destructive than the riots. I think the riots brought the fire department together and the strike pulled them apart. During the riots we didn't have one firehouse that had any damage to the communications equipment or anything else. We had shots fired at us, but no one broke in. No one stripped the firehouses. During the strike, we had officers' cars that were damaged. We had communications equipment that was pulled out. We had hose that was pulled off apparatus. Very damaging and I think that was a watershed for discipline on the Newark Fire Department.

The firemen went on strike against the officers. I was president of the officers. We used to let the firemen go in and negotiate first and hold back. Then we would go in and say, "Okay, we want a percentage over the firemen." Make life easy. That happened this year. We got a promise of say five percent, whatever it was. Tony Imperiale stirred the firemen up, that they got screwed by the officers. He was councilman at the time. The next thing I know, the firemen are agitating for a strike. Some of my guys were coming to me saying we should support the firemen. I said, "That's real easy pal. If you vote to strike, you get a new president because I'm not going on strike. I've taken an oath. I take my oath seriously. I don't believe in strikes."

At the time I had a couple of salvage men who worked for me. I was in the Fifth Battalion and they were old timers with had no civil service protection. So, they stayed. I wouldn't let them ride. I said, "You guys, I don't want you riding. You won't, just the officers." I had Hogan's Army there. Captains who hadn't pulled a length of hose in, Christ, twenty years. But at least they all came to work.

They had the picket line across the street, including my driver who was out there picketing. I was at Twenty-seven at the time. They formed a pretty good wedge around our firehouse. So, I walked over to them and said, "Look guys, I don't want any trouble. I don't want anybody to get hurt, but I'm telling you one thing. If you see the doors open, we're coming out and we're going to whatever fire we're going to. I expect you to part your picket line peacefully and allow us to come through." "Well, what if we don't?" "Well, we'll get to that point later, but I'm responding to any fire alarm that comes into this station." "Well, that's bull shit." My driver

Vinnie steps out and says, "You better listen to him because he'll do it." He was the voice of reason. The bell came in and off we went. No one did any damage to our station.

I also had a guy who worked for me at the time who asked for the day off because the strike was coming up. He knew the strike was coming up at that time. I gave him a personal day, so he wasn't counted as AWOL that time. Yet, he went around and threatened other firefighters to walk out. The first night back after the strike, we're going on our rounds. I said to Vinnie, "Park the car here." "Why?" I said, "Park the car here." Took my shirt off, threw it in the car, walked into the firehouse. I said to him, "I want to talk to you outside." I said, "I don't have any rank on. It's just me and you out here. I'm going to tell you something. You get out of my battalion. I don't want you working for me, any place close to me. And if you don't think I'm serious, come and get a piece of me. We're both about the same age and I'll knock your ass one end of this alley to the next." I turned around and walked out. This guy really hurt me. Here's a coward, takes a personal day so he doesn't get charged AWOL and then goes around threatening other people. And I might add he's another Irishman, which made it doubly hurt.

So, I think the strike was a blow to the discipline of the Newark Fire Department that Newark never recovered from because I knew guys who were my neighbors. When the firefighters first started the peaceful picketing, my neighbors said, "That's a good idea." But then they just kept growing in intensity. There was an incident with a bus downtown where they knocked a window in on a bus. It was bad.

But it only lasted twenty-four hours. Of course, I was doubly involved because I was president of the officers' at the time. I literally organized the officers into firefighting squads. Not one officer refused. No one pulled the bullshit of I'm on sick leave or whatever. They all did what they were supposed to do. Surprised me, it really did. It's a moral conflict. I have to work with these guys and ba ba boom. Most guys turned out.

McGee: The strike, the strike was another very terrible time. I mean a terrible time. It was terrible, but it was good in the sense that it made the city start to believe these guys are serious. Now we were very fortunate to have a guy like John Caufield as a director. That's my opinion. He could have done a lot more to us had he wanted to. We are also fortunate that we had the cooperation of men who had time on the job, because it was very easy for a guy who had one year on the job to say let's strike. Facing the possibility of dismissal, well he would lose one year out of his life. But it's another thing when a vast majority of these guys who had fifteen, twenty years on the job cooperated with the strike.

Nobody wanted to strike and I'm certainly not proud of it. Neither is anybody else I've spoken to, but these guys literally put their jobs on the line and their families' welfare on the line because they had twenty years to lose. Suppose he reacted the way Reagan did as President. "Okay, everyone's fired." I'm serious. It certainly could have happened. It didn't happen in large part because of Caufield. Now, Caufield was no dope. Not everybody loved him. His job wasn't to have everybody love him. He had to answer to certain people, but he was a man who had a heart, whether you liked him or not. I think he was a major reason we didn't suffer more severely.

The fourth tour was working days as I remember it and they had to walk out of the firehouse at a certain time like three o'clock or four o'clock and we were due in. We didn't come in and the fourth tour went out. The beautiful part about it was it was about eighty-five or ninety percent effective. The firehouses were almost abandoned. Only through the grace of God or whatever you want to call it, there were no major fires in that like thirty-six hour period when we were on strike. It lasted about a day and a half.

Finally Mayor Addonizio said, "Anybody who's not back to work by noon is fired." Then through the phone call or whatever method they had of corresponding to each other, we were able to get everybody back to work. After that we had a big meeting. Everybody was ordered to the council chamber in City Hall, all the fire department. Caufield got up and gave his talk. He said, "I haven't made up my mind what I'm going to do to you guys yet." He didn't say he wasn't going to do anything. He just let it die. He just hung that little piece of cheese out. He had that if you stepped out of line again.

It was a relief to go back to work, because nobody really wanted that strike. But had it not been for strike, the young guys on this job today wouldn't have the benefits we have. We have great benefits. When you retire, you see it even more. We're very fortunate and we have to attribute that to the proposals put together by the union guys. I wasn't too happy with a lot of our leaders, but they must have done something right. I mean we should be grateful.

As far as the strike itself, there were some comical sides to it, too. I remember the strike meeting when everybody would be up hollering for a strike, strike, strike. Then we had the strike. One guy called me almost in tears asking me, "What are we going to do?" Hey, wait a minute. You were at that meeting weren't you? You were one of the guys up there hollering for a strike. Didn't you expect them to respond? I mean, what's the matter? If you make an action, somebody's going to respond to that action? Now that they're responding to the action, you're going to fall. Now is the time you have to stand up.

It worked out, but that was absolutely the beginning of them starting to understand that we needed better ways of handling our problems. It could have been really disastrous if it wasn't for Caufield. It was a hard time, a very tense time. I had just bought my house and hadn't even made my first mortgage payment. My wife and I literally lost a couple of nights sleep. It was scary because you didn't know what would happen. The guys came out in front of the Prosecutor's Office with the subpoenas. They were giving you subpoenas that told you if you weren't back on the job by noon, you were fired. You took the thing and didn't go back to work. One fellow who didn't strike told me his reasons and certainly I couldn't disagree with his reasons, morally and so forth. The only thing I said to him was, "Okay, suppose they get the money. Are you going to give your part back?" Of course he wouldn't do that, so I said, "You have to understand their part, too." I was part of the other part. "We have these misgivings also, you know, about whether it's moral, whether it's right, or if somebody dies and so on and so forth. But if the other side's not playing ball at all, we're forced into this situation."

It was a very, very difficult time. It was difficult in some firehouses. I was very fortunate. We had a good officer who understood that he had to do what he had to do and we had to do what we had to do. That wasn't the case in every firehouse. It caused a lot of friction between the officers and the men, in weaker firehouses I would say. But that was a rough time.

Stoffers: I was up in the Academy at the time. One of the Battalion Chiefs in the second battalion was out on sick leave. Redden called me up and told me to get down there and work the Second Battalion. I went down when they had the strike. Iannuzzi was on the fourth tour then. He was going to stay in the firehouse and I was going to go out in the car.

We went out to make the rounds and nothing happened. We picked everything up, came back to the firehouse. Then we get a call that the guys in the fireboat would stay in the fireboat, but they won't go and work in another firehouse on a detail. I said to whoever was driving me at the time, "Let's take a ride up to the fireboat." Dolak was the Deputy Chief. He told me to go up and see what it's about.

We pull up in front of Two Engine. Valent was the captain there and he was running across the street. He said, "Some of the guys on strike are in the kitchen." I said, "What?" He said, "Yes, these guys are in there telling all the guys to get out of the firehouse." So I said, "Did you tell them recall is on?" He said, "No." I get out of the car and go across the street and told them recall was on and they could go up to Eleven Engine. They didn't want to go. Valent put it in the book with all their names and everything.

I went down to the boat. The guys down there were saying, "We'll stay here, but we don't want to be detailed to somebody else's firehouse." So, I said, "Well, if you stay here, you stay here." He says, "Could we get something to eat." I said, "Yes, you can get something, sure." So they went out to get something to eat, but they never came back.

Then I went back to the firehouse and I told Dolak what happened up at Two Engine. I think this was a Friday night. I come in Monday morning and I get a call from Redden to come over to headquarters. I go over and Dolak is sitting there. Dolak told Redden everything I had told him. Redden said, "Well, you're going to have to put these guys on charges." I made up a report, told him what happened, and Joyce typed up all the charges. But I understood nothing ever happened, nothing ever came of it because Addonizio supposedly gave everybody a pardon for what happened.

I was at a picnic this past July and one of the guys involved asked me, "Remember that thing that happened during the strike?" I said, "Yes." He said, "You know we got three days suspension? Didn't bother me, I went out iron working." I hear there were other incidents that happened in other places and nothing was ever done about it. Somebody who was in tight with the powers that be, they just forgot about.

McGrory: There was a strike, but I happened to be lucky. I think I was on vacation. I was in New England at my brother's and I was so happy. They did some stupid things. A Battalion Chief at the time got his tires cut. That was an individual with a gripe. Some men did things against a particular officer because they had that opportunity to take out their gripes. Some of the men involved at the time weren't the best firefighters in the world either.

What else could we do? They push you in a corner so much. I don't believe in strikes in our type of job. You can't. Who's going to protect the people? But without the unions we would have been in bad shape.

Denvir: I was in Eleven Engine at the time, but I was on vacation during the strike. It was something that I guess had to be done. Most of the guys didn't want to do it, but they did it because they were all stand up guys. I don't think I would have crossed the picket line if I had to. If they were picketing in front, I wouldn't have gone in. I said, "Thank God I was on vacation and they didn't get hold of me." I met Jackie Drew, who was Chief Drew's son, on the boardwalk down in Point Pleasant. He said, "Wacky, what are you doing? You're supposed to be back at work. There's a recall in. All officers have to go back." I says, "Really, I don't know anything about that." He says, "You better call." I says, "Come on, will you. You have to be kidding. All right, I'm calling." I called the operator. He says,

"You better get your ass in here." I says, "What are you talking about. I want to talk to somebody in the firehouse." "You can't." Because you had to call headquarters then, you couldn't dial directly to the firehouse. I just laughed and put the phone down. There were a lot of bitter feelings that came out for some people.

Freda: When the strike occurred I was working as a captain in the Rescue Squad. When all the firemen went on strike or the great majority anyway, the officers were asked to man the rigs and ride with the rigs. Now several peculiar things happened. By and large most of the firemen, most of them, stayed home and were very uncomfortable about going on strike. My feelings were that if you really would take a confidential poll, you would find out that a large per cent of them would not even have gone on strike. They did it because everyone else did it and because the union told them to do it. In fact, the union felt very uncomfortable about it after a while and I'll prove my point in a second.

I rode on the Rescue Squad. Now I started hearing the stories, especially in Fifteen Engine on Park Avenue that some of the firemen started hanging outside the firehouses. There were a couple of fistfights between firemen and a captain in Fifteen Engine. One fireman was literally knocked out by a captain. We're only human beings and we started wondering when we were going to be attacked because we were riding. There was one captain driving the Rescue rig; there's one sitting in the front; and there're two of us in the back of the Rescue rig. I started hearing stories about firemen planning to jump in the rigs and beat up the captains. That might have been just talk at the time, but it was wise to be prudent. In fact, I even went so far as carrying a black jack in my pocket. Some of these firemen are quite big and I didn't want to entertain the fact that one of them was going to beat me up. I wasn't going to allow it to happen.

The odd thing was there were a couple of fires that occurred during the strike. Firemen showed up at the fires and a couple of them pitched in to help. There were situations where they pulled the hose off the rig and made it hard for you to operate. But on the other end of the spectrum, there were actually firemen around who went to the fire and they even helped out. Because a lot of them were still visible in the city, they were wandering around in cars. The buffs were chased out of the firehouse because they came in to ride. They were told not to hang around the firehouse because they were scabbing the job. So all these fire buffs, the auxiliary firefighting force, disappeared from the scene. They were no help to you at all. But the fires were put out.

The strike didn't go on too long. Because I remember the union president called me at the Rescue Squad and said to me that he just got notice from the mayor that if the firefighters weren't back to duty by eight o'clock the next morning, he was going to fire every one of them. His direction to me was that I was to try and contact all the members of the Rescue Squad and tell them to get into work immediately, by eight o'clock tomorrow morning. He didn't want to make all the phone calls, so he was calling the individual houses. I guess he was concerned about it, too. He might have been relieved. I don't know. He didn't put up a big fight. I did call the members up and none of them procrastinated. They all came back quite rapidly because my feelings were they felt very foolish and they were very concerned about someone dying in a fire. They were on strike, but I think the great majority of them were more than happy to come back to work. It wasn't in their nature really to be on strike with fires occurring in the city.

But there were some bad incidents that did ensue.   I was at a testimonial honoring a person making Battalion Chief and right in the middle of the ceremony this fireman got up and started to lambast the Battalion Chief.   His name was Chief Stoffers now that I recall and this fireman got up and lambasted him in front of everyone at the racket. I don't want to use the language that he used of course because he used a lot of vulgarities.   The essence of it was that he was put on charges because something had happened over near Two Engine; some very severe harassment that this fireman did and then Chief Stoffers put him on charges. But I have to hand it to the newly appointed chief because most of the people in the audience were very embarrassed for the honoree at the testimonial. The guy shouting didn't get any sympathy. Most of us felt very uncomfortable and felt great sympathy for this man standing up here and being interrupted by this guy hollering out obscenities. People were trying to shut him up and I remember Chief Stoffers saying, "No, let him talk. He has a right to speak. And I have no problem with him saying what he wants to say." I admired him for it, that's why I remember it.   This man went on for several minutes. When he was done, the ceremony continued on.

What I'm trying to express is there were a lot of hard feelings between the officers and the men from this strike. We had no choice because the officer's union was not on strike. We had to work because we had no protection. It would have been silly for us. We were all in sympathy with the men, but no officer as I can recall participated in the strike.   Our officers' union told us, "We won't protect you. We're not condoning the strike or anything."

Charpentier: I believe the union contract was involved in the strike. That's when they ordered us back to the firehouse to work overtime and we weren't doing it. There was a lot of confusion. A lot of the captains were calling up people and really insulting the families of the firemen. They were using very choice words. "Get in or else." Not such polite words, but very rough, harsh words. I know for a fact, this one captain who was in Six Engine at the time, really laid it into my wife. I wouldn't even use that kind of language on another fireman in the firehouse with a real heated argument.

I was off those two days, but then when I was called in, I was scheduled to come in anyway. A lot of fellows really rebelled. They refused to come in on anything but their regular time. It was a bitter time there for quite a while between some officers and the firemen. It wasn't all the officers because the majority of them were gentlemen about it. But there were a few rebels who thought they were going to win the war with their actions and their language. It wound up in the end that they were the ones who really got hurt. When I first came on the job I was told by a chief officer, "You make me look good. I don't make you look good."

Dunn: The strike was back in the seventies and was only by the firefighters. The officers in the fire department at that time did not participate in the strike. It was probably no more than, if I can remember correctly, a twenty-four hour type of strike. Then there was an injunction by the courts and people were ordered back to work by the judges and they complied. What caused that was the failure of the city to negotiate in good faith with our people at the time and the salaries had dropped back to a very low scale.

I believe Artie Braggart was the president at the time. He was a young firefighter who said if you're going to get ahead and try to improve this job, you'd better be ready to take risks. They took a big risk that time. That's been adjudicated. The wounds between the officers' union and the firefighters came to a conclusion fairly quickly. There were very few disciplinary charges filed by the city against the union members. People weren't home on sick leave or refused to go to doctors. When a Superior Court got involved and ordered the members back or they were going to imprison the union president, everybody complied in a fairly quick and orderly manner.

On a personal note, I called each one of my crew members when I was a captain at Twelve Engine at the time and told them that the strike had been settled and that they had twenty-four hours to be ready for the next shift. It always amused me that they weren't sure I was telling them the truth or if this was another gimmick of the officers' union having a little foray with the firefighters union. But when we sat down the next night, there was no animosity. They were there. They did check with their union to verify that this was the court order. I don't remember any animosity in the company I was in on any of the tours concerning the strike other than there was something necessary at the time. The members did what the union requested them to do which was to go on strike. Some people felt very bad about it initially, but after the first couple of hours and the quick conclusion to the strike, it didn't have any lasting effect on anything. And we did do fine later on in negotiations. So, it did have a good effect from the negotiating part of that.

I wasn't on duty during the strike, but we had a recall of all officers. I believe I wound up in Twenty Engine and I worked there for several hours. By the time we were called in it was late at night and by the time the day trick was due to change the settlement was there. The members were ordered back by court and they had complied.

Carragher: We had the strike when I was in Six Engine. The firemen went on strike. I happened to be the working captain that night when the strike happened. I think it was myself, Bobby King who was a captain in Six Engine, and John Ryan. The three of us were Six Engine crew that night.

Haran: Oh, the strike was there. Yes, and I'll tell you what, that was a bad time. There was fireman against fireman that time, firemen against officers. I was on Park Avenue at that time. When it came down that we were going to go on strike everybody sighed. We didn't know what to do because we couldn't strike. Everybody was going to be fired. We were threatened. I was only on the job about five years or something, six years. So, everybody was hoping it wasn't their tour that had to walk out that day. When a tour walked out, we thought what was going to happen was that it was only going to last a few hours. They would capitulate and everybody would be back. It didn't happen that way. They walked out and it went on.

The officers were in a different union, so they had all the officers come in. All the captains had to work. Everybody was nervous that it was going to be their tour that leads because a lot of guys wouldn't do it. I think it was the third tour that walked out that day. Now the firemen are mad at the officers. Some firemen were getting pissed off at other firemen. Some men called in sick leave that morning because they knew the strike was going to take place. So, rather than walk out of the firehouse, they're going to play the sharp guy and call in sick that morning. They thought they were being cool. They were because they escaped it anyhow because it was a technicality. How are you going to prove you were sick or not? But it didn't look good in the eyes of the other guys who had to walk out, their brother firemen.

There were vigilante groups forming. Not only that, there was a guy out in front of Park Avenue hollering at one of the captains, "You scab." This captain wasn't a guy to take that lightly. He was a big guy himself. He came out. Big fist fight out on Park Avenue. The captain decked this guy, but he hit him a sucker shot and the guy went back after him. Alarm systems were cut in the street. When the companies went out of the firehouses, guys went in. The so-called vigilante groups were pulling the wires out of the desk bell because you could open the back of them. That's why they're all locked now, but back then you could go in there and pull all the batteries out and pull all the wires out. No alarms could come into the firehouse. That was a serious thing to do back then. It was crazy to do it.

These were the things that were done to get certain things that firemen enjoy today because as bad as it was, it got us certain things. The city wouldn't want that repeated and they didn't like when it happened then. But certain things got accomplished out of that. Here today they're giving things up, but these guys don't realize that because that's two generations ago or at least one generation ago. So those things are forgotten about.

Cahill: The strike was one of my memorable experiences. We went on strike one night. We did it very reluctantly. I remember myself and Kevin Mahon sitting down in his backyard on Magazine Street with about three minutes to six, we still hadn't made up our minds. I think we both knew it was wrong, but I think the final decision came down to if enough of us do it, they can't hang all of us. That helped.

The general feeling was nobody wanted to do it. I felt it wasn't right. Many people didn't think it was right to do. It was just kind of peer pressure. They didn't want to hurt somebody else. You were torn. You knew your obligation was to the citizens. You didn't want to hurt them. You didn't want to hurt your fellow firefighters either. It was a real tough decision to make and I still think it was wrong. I would never do it again. It was very bitter and took the department years to heal. That was something we had to do. I don't feel very proud that it went that way. It only lasted one night.

There were no fires. It was like somebody threw a switch in the city. There were a lot of false alarms. In this case it was the firemen. The officers were supposed to go out with us and they didn't go. They went in, which caused a lot of hard feelings. There were incidents around some of the firehouses that were really nasty. It just didn't make it look very professional. The city really could have hung us. I guess, fortunately, it was a new election, a new mayor. He came in and wiped the slate clean, dropped all the charges against us. But he could have done a lot more to us than he did.

We lost a lot of prestige or confidence with the public. The public was very angry at us for going out. I can't blame them. It was an indefensible thing, to sit there and tell some taxpayer that you weren't going to come to his house at night if it caught fire because you didn't get a pay raise; it's very difficult to defend, to get across. But we survived it.

Butler: I was a union officer at the time of the strike. Received a hand delivered subpoena, a court order not to strike, delivered to my home. I was named to that suit. All of us, everybody who was an elected union officer was named in that suit. During the strike, I went to the union office. I was on the last day of my seventy-two the first day of the strike. I went to the union office and primarily assisted the president down there fielding phone calls. Maybe riding out with someone to firehouses, our big thing was we didn't want to get guys in trouble fighting with civilians or with fellow firefighters who weren't going to honor the strike. We wanted to try to keep everything peaceful. We wanted a strong showing, but peaceful. That's what I did and the next day I just went down and sat across the street from the firehouse, refused to go in.

That night, the court order was put out, the second court order holding the union officers in contempt. Then each individual who refused to show up for work would be held in contempt of the court and would be fined and punished. Word came out about midnight that night that everybody should report to work the next day. So, we had a lot of maneuvering around to do to get the guys to go to work immediately. We sat at several phones calling individuals due in the next day to tell them to come to work. They knew who we were and "Hey, come to work, go to work tomorrow morning."

We struck because of the city's refusal to negotiate with us on any kind of a contract, their refusal to even sit. It was over a long period of time. It wasn't just, "Well we're not sitting with you." It was over a long period of time. They refused to deal with us before binding arbitration. They just refused to sit with us, to give us anything. "No, you're not getting anything period." No raise, no benefits, nothing, take a walk. At the time they had the power to do that. They weren't forced to sit with you. And just the way they acted, "Oh no, we're not going to deal with you."

State monies were promised, but initially they said, "You on the fire department aren't getting anything anyway." was a comment out of city hall in Newark. But the state monies weren't coming that day. It was down the line a little bit. "Well, you know we want x number of dollars of state money." The union president demanded. "No, you aren't getting any of that state money." We have to do something to change your mind. Bump. But this was a refusal for them really to talk with us at all, deal with anything.

Then with the strike, what lots of guys did during the strike, I know for a fact, they had their turnout gear with them in the cars and if they saw an apparatus they'd follow it at a little bit of a distance. If there was a major fire those guys would have bailed out of their cars to work, but not ride on an apparatus or respond out of a firehouse or anything. It was just very fortunate during that time there were very, very few fires.

There were a lot of things going on, guys coming to work and other guys stopping them outside, "Where are you going?" "Well, I don't believe in the strike." There were roughed up situations. There were officers going in the firehouses and the men harassing them outside. There were some firemen in the firehouses that were kind of asked, "Well, maybe you should leave." They didn't leave and nobody was looking and they got a little closer message. By and large there wasn't that much over all violence. Ninety-nine percent of what went on was verbal.

There were some probationary firefighters and they were told to report to work. There were some at the time and they were told definitely report to work. That was well thought out and planned. Each one of them was personally contacted by a union officer and told regardless of what you hear anybody doing, you report to work.

Wargo: I remember the strike. It didn't last too long and it didn't amount to much. They had a court order to go back to work or lose your job. Even though the guys were out on strike, a few of them still went to fires, so it really didn't matter. I think it gave more ill will than it did anything else for the little bit of time. It was one of the rare times in the history of the fire department where people had perhaps a little sour taste in their mouth.

Chapter Three: Firehouse Differences

Redden: I never ran into any ethnic friction. You know the Italians came on and they got into the department just like the Irish did. You hear stories, but that's not my recollection, that there was any problem as far as nationality.

Kinnear: Before my time I think there was friction between groups. I think that when the Italians started to go on the department, there was animosity by the Irish against them. I don't think it was as much as the change when the blacks began to come on. I heard stories there was, but never saw it myself. I went to Six Engine and we had an old German guy named Teddy Smith; we had an Englishman; and we had Irish; and we had Frenchman Fredette. We all got along. We had arguments, but nothing about ethnics that's for sure. We had arguments over other things.

 The first blacks who came on the job, I think they were pretty decent. They did the job. There were people who were prejudiced against them. Who wouldn't sleep in the same bed with them or sit down and have a cup of coffee with them, but I think most of the guys accepted them.

Masters: When I went in, the predominant ethnic group was Irish, Irish and German. The Germans, we got along. There was one guy. He used to talk about guineas and wops and all that shit. I didn't let it bother me. But the next year, we get Perdesco. He looked just like Kojak. So, we're at the table eating one time and this guy is spouting off about the guineas and wops. Perdesco jumps up. He says, "What did you say, guinea and wop?" And he said, "You, you're another one. Why the hell you cook Italian food for these fucks? If they want spaghetti, let them eat it out of a can. And you, I'll take you outside right now." That was the end of guinea and wops.

And here was a guy who didn't bother anybody. All ethnic groups went through discrimination.

F. Grehl: There wasn't too much friction among my age group, the veterans who came out of the service. We were used to that in the service. I never heard the word discrimination all through high school. I went to West Side High School and there were blacks there on the ball team, blacks in the classes. Never heard anything about racism or anything, didn't hear it in the service until after the war. Now I started to hear it when the war ended because I ended up in an all-Southern outfit. Of course they hated the blacks. That's when I saw this prejudice as far as blacks went. It didn't make any difference whether they were good, bad, or indifferent. They hated them. But we didn't have it among ourselves. The old timers probably had a little prejudice, those who weren't prepared for it. But I think we straightened that out quick. "Hey, the guy does the job; I don't care what he is."

Of course, when Willie Thomas, the first black, came on the job everybody was very, very much in arms. Who's going to get him? Nobody wanted him. In 1959 when I got promoted to captain, we went to the four tours. That's when quite a few more blacks came on. Where are they going to put them? Well, the unions had the power then, too. "We work with you," the politicians. "You work with us. These are the houses that are giving us the trouble, all the fellows in these houses." Twenty-nine Engine/Ten Truck was one of them. Belmont Avenue was another. So, they loaded them up. That's when the problems occurred. Willie Thomas was alone. We had Richie Freeman. He was in Twelve Engine. There were the Evelyn brothers, Curtis Moore, and Charlie Chapman. One was in Seventeen. One was in Twelve. There was absolutely no real problem. In fact, JanTausch was one of the ones who volunteered as a captain. He took the first blacks down there. Two out of the four people he had were black. JanTausch didn't have any trouble with them. Most of the people didn't have any trouble with them, if they were halfway decent people. But you had bad ones. You had some who would test you to no extent. "I don't want them sleeping in my bed." If a black came into the company there was a bed assigned for them. That's where the prejudice was building. There's nothing like that today. They may still feel bad about it, but they don't have special beds or anything like that anymore. You learn to live with it. You get over it.

McCormack: I was never involved in any of that ethnic stuff. I think people tend, in some cases perhaps, to be clannish and stick together. But I don't know if there was a real policy or anything of that nature. In fact, I know it wasn't a policy because I worked with people of various nationalities. I don't think the fact that I was Irish ever had anything to do with where I was assigned. I don't believe it did.

Baldino: In the early days of our department it didn't hurt to be Irish or German and there were houses that didn't want to change. Engine Eleven/Truck Eleven still wanted to remain Irish and Engine Six still wanted to remain German. When I was running for the Relief Association, a member of Engine Eleven took me out side and said, "You're okay for an Italian. The guys are going to give you the vote anyway." I had to use discretion in my answer and it wasn't thank you. This was in 1963. You would think that just coming out of a world war, this would stop because most of the guys were ex-servicemen.

Wall: There were a lot of Irish obviously, Germans, a good number of Italians. When I came on the job there was one black guy, Willie Thomas. Then a black guy named Shelly Harris came on with me. So, in '54 there were two black guys, Willie Thomas and Shelly Harris. We didn't see a lot more black guys until the forty-two hours when I think something like eight or ten black guys were appointed.

Freeman: There was one captain who was Irish and he was *Irish*. He didn't like Italians and he didn't like blacks. He always gave me a hard time. He gave Rosetti, Captain Rosetti, a hard time. We had Jimmy Murray when he first came on the job. He gave Jimmy Murray a hard time, ran him out of the firehouse. He was just terrible. Nobody liked him either. When he retired they didn't even give him a party. They didn't say boo to him. He just left. I understand when I wasn't around it was nigger this, nigger that, nigger this. A couple of guys told me this. I kind of stayed away from him.

We had a couple of confrontations. He used to get on me about not shaving. I used to say, "Well, Cap, I don't shave that often. When I shave too much my face gets raw. I have to let it grow out." So we got to the point where I told him I wasn't going to shave. And he called the chief down a couple of times. One time he called the chief down about reliefs. They told me that there were only three guys coming in, so I left. He jumped on me the following day I worked. "You're not supposed to leave until you're properly relieved." I said, "Look, Cap, they said one man was on vacation, so the extra guy could go." He was real ticklish about the reliefs, the rules and regulations, and all that stuff. I think he put me on the book a couple of nights for that. Then he found out I was right and he apologized.

That was the second time he apologized to me, which I give him credit for. He was wrong and he admitted it. But still he used to jump on me and all the Italians and blacks. He used to talk about them. One time a city worker came in to do some work and he was at the table talking about Italians, wop this, wop that. This painter says, "You say that one more time and I'm going to punch you out." He stopped that stuff. After a while he wouldn't say it. We were all going to put in for transfers out of Twelve Engine because of him. Jimmy Wiggins did put in. He went to Five Truck. Right after that this captain retired. I don't think he was going to, but because of the problem that he was having he got out. He came from Fifteen Engine on a bet. "I bet you don't go to Twelve Engine." He came over on a bet that he wouldn't come to Twelve Engine.

There are times prejudice goes to the fire ground. It's happened a few times. I know of one incident and I've heard of others. I think it was racial. It was between two captains. The chief asked one company to go up and relieve another on a line. The captain on the line didn't want to give it up, an argument ensued and then fisticuffs. I think it was stupid. The one guy just had to say "Okay" and walk downstairs. It would have been finished. But he's a hot head and the captain on the line is a hot head. I don't know if he's a racist or what. I've heard different things. That may have been part of it. It may not have been part of it. He didn't want to give the line up. The other captain said, "Well, the chief said I should take the line." He didn't give up. They are both captains and they started fighting. I don't know how it broke up. The chief took care of it verbally. But that's the kind of stuff that spills over on the fire ground.

My guys were involved in one thing. We were over in NJIT* one day and one of my guys asked an engine guy to do something and the guy started cursing at him. So I would imagine that was part of the racial thing because all my guys are black now. So I told my guy, "Hey, forget about it." I'm not one of those guys who fights about things and screams and

---

* New Jersey Institute of Technology

jumps up and down. Most of the guys know me. They know I'm not that way. There are guys who probably don't say anything to me.

I've lost some friendships because of this captain's thing. We had a suit with the city for almost ten years on the captain's test in '79. I never talked about it, but some of the white guys found out about it somehow and they stopped talking to me. That was the end of it. They stopped talking to me. I was wondering what happened. Then it occurred to me, they probably knew that we have a suit against the city for this captain's exam. I had a pretty good rapport with everybody. I even talked to guys who wouldn't talk to me. I'd say hello to guys and all of the sudden these guys wouldn't say anything to me.

There were times I would walk over to Five Truck and I'd say, "Hey, guys" and nobody says anything. That's embarrassing. I mean, what's wrong with me? A guy I had been talking to for years did a flip-flop. In the beginning when he first came on the job, he was pretty broadminded, but then a few years later he started to go down. I've heard him talk about blacks and certain names were said when he got angry at what was happening on the job. Why stop talking to me because I'm trying to do something for myself or you might say quote unquote for my race? Try to better my position and also help out my brothers and sisters. That's not the first time a suit's been filed. Whether it was you or whether it's me, a suit's a suit. It just happens that I'm trying to do something as a black that may affect you. That's why they didn't like it.

When they came up with the new type exam and they canned that captain's test that they had; that was even worse. There were threats against black guys. I'm going to throw you off a roof. Don't let me catch you at a fire. I mean I heard this. Nobody said it directly to me. Then more guys stopped talking to me and probably other guys, too. So I just went along with it. You don't want to talk to me, fine. Somewhere along the line you're going to have to say something to me.

I made captain. We had the suit. It was settled. Then they came up with the percentage figures in the exam. Now a lot of guys didn't like that, which I could understand that too. I could understand that, sure. If it were going to affect me, I would think about it, too. But then you have to look at the whole picture, this whole racial thing, this whole discrimination thing. How it got started. You have to go back to slavery times when these things happened and how blacks were kept down and couldn't do anything. Whichever way we turned, we couldn't go anywhere. The results of all that was this new type exam and percentage figures. I've heard nasty remarks and the whole nine yards. You hear stories about this, that, or the other thing, guys talking. You walk into a room with a whole bunch of white guys and all of the sudden the room gets quiet. So, you know after a while you don't want to be bothered anymore. Not that I hate anybody. I don't. It's just that there's no understanding.

I would say it's racial first, but it's also economic. It's definitely economic. If I get promoted I'm going to make more money. That's better for my family, but if a white person took the job there wouldn't be much said about it. When a black person takes the job away from me? No way, no way. He's not smart enough. He's dumb. That's another thing. They think we can't handle certain jobs, but that's a myth also. Because you have dumb white guys and you have dumb black guys. So, why pick on the black guy because he's dumb. You have dumb white captains. You have dumb black captains. Where do you draw the line? All you see is black and that's all you see. You have tunnel vision. You don't see anything else.

As far as the bitterness it's created, it's probably going to take a generation to get over it. I won't be around. It's just going to continue. I feel that education is a key with this. I think people have to be educated to know what they're up against when it comes to black people. There's a certain history that's going to have to be given to the white man in order for him to understand why the blacks are going through this and why we're jumping up and down. I'm not saying we should jump up and down. I think that we should stop crying, as blacks, about certain things. Hey, let's not cry racial prejudice. Let's get out here and get an education and try to do the best we can.

Yes, you're going to run up against prejudice all the time. As long as we're here it's going to happen. When it's going to stop? Nobody knows. But if you're going to be out there and if you do a good job, then you're not going to look so bad. But if you do a bad job, you're going to look bad because you're black. But the white man, when he does a bad job, they don't look at him. That's because we've always been looked down on and whenever we do something wrong it's like an explosion. When the white man does a bad job, it's like a firecracker. You know what I mean. That's a good analogy. In other words they see us and they don't see you.

Education is the only way. You might say have classes on why are blacks the way they are and why we're jumping up and down. Why we're demanding certain things. I think we should stop some of it in a way. Let's get on with life. Let's stop hollering black this, black that. This is discrimination; this is discrimination, discrimination, discrimination. You're going to have to get over it somehow. The better you're educated, the better job that you do, the less I think there's going to be discrimination and racism. And they're going to look at you in a different light. Oh, this guy. He does a good job. Without saying, "That black guy does a good job." They're just going to say, "Yes, he does a good job." But it's always going to be black and white.

I don't get around to all these things and I don't listen to all these things, but I would say in a way it has improved on the fire department because there are more of us. And I think there's an education there in the different types, different personalities of guys. Some guys are tough and other guys aren't. I think there should be a better mix in the fire department. Mix it with whites and blacks rather than have all black companies and all white companies. Hey, you can have those, too. I don't think they want to do that. But there I think you have to put the right people together. You can't just throw people in together like that, black and white because some guys don't like that. You have to be aware of that. I wouldn't do that.

But it's gotten a little bit better because we're here and there's nothing anybody can do about it. So the white guys are going to have to learn how to get along with the black guys and vise-versa. Yes, we're different than you are. No, we don't always cause trouble. Yes, you are in drugs and yes, we are in drugs. There's no difference. It's just the color of the skin. And what you've heard a long time ago doesn't have to be. You live in a black area, naturally and you live in a white area, there's a difference in the way you live and what you see. I don't want to live there. You know all the black people and a black person would say, "Hey, I don't want to live with all those white people." It's the same thing from both sides. Everybody is looking at it in one way. You're not looking at it and trying to understand the other guy.

Even bigoted guys acknowledge when you do a good job on the fire ground. When there's a fire, everyone pulls together. Then after the fire it goes back again. I think that's true from what I've seen. Because I know a lot of guys have talked about my guys. You know these guys are good firefighters. You have a bunch of good guys there. But then, aside from that, I think it goes back the other way. Everybody works as a team at the fire. Now behind that mask you don't know who it is, but if you know that Twelve Engine is all black and you see a Twelve on their helmet, right away, you're marked.

Now there's a difference. You're on that stairway with me. You're not going to let me by. You're going to have that, "Twelve Engine is black. I don't want this black guy to get ahead of me." See, guys think like that. Whereas if they don't know who are you in the dark and they don't ask, "Who are you? Where are you from?" If you're just working side-by-side trying to put a fire out, there is no difference. You don't know who that guy is, but you guys are working together to put that fire out.

Once you get down to the end of the hall and you go into that room and you take your mask off. "Oh, wow, this guy's good. I didn't know he was black." Maybe he didn't know you were black because you were going down the hall with him and fighting that fire and both of you ended up in the same room together. When you took your masks off, here you are black and white. I think he had a little more respect for you then; knowing that you did just as good a job as he did. He has a different outlook on you, on blacks, because of that.

McGee: The department was mostly Irish and Italian. By that time the German influence had sort of started to wane. I imagine prior to me coming on it was probably mostly German and Irish and then it became Irish and Italian and then it became pretty much anybody. Then little by little the black and the Puerto Rican/Spanish element started to come on the job. But when I first came on it was primarily Irish and Italian.

Central Avenue was an Irish firehouse, but I don't know if you couldn't get in there because you weren't Irish. Probably being Irish helped me, but I had no connections with anybody and I wouldn't have cared less where I went really. There was nothing going on that was anti-anybody else. It just happened that an Irish guy knew another guy's son was coming on the job or something. They'd probably call whoever they could call to try to get him assigned there.

McGrory: In the '50s when I came on, there were blacks on the fire department. They took the same test. There were blacks in the New York City Police Department who were detectives and had pretty high rank in the '30s. In these cities a lot of people in minority groups didn't go for these jobs and the fire department in particular. They probably opted for the police department or something like that. They wouldn't come on the fire department. The fire department's a tough job that a lot of people didn't want.

When they got on the job it was different. The fire department shows you what the thinking was in the country as a whole or in the city as a whole. And the fire department was no different than that thinking. The attitudes of the Director or the Chiefs or whoever it was, were about the same as the community's.

Denvir: When I went to Twelve Engine I had Sal DeFranco, Boisy Cosby, Bobby Bennis, and Curtis Moore. So, it was a mixed crew, two blacks and two whites. They were good, good guys.

There wasn't really any animosity between them. Curtis was bitter. He never drove until I got there. I told him, "You drive." He was glad. He wanted to drive. I guess the previous captain wouldn't let him drive. But Curtis was good. He was in good shape. I remember a couple of days in the projects when the elevators were gone. He'd say, "I've got it, Cap." he'd take the radio, run up the stairs, and see what it was. Everybody else would just take their time going up. He'd come down, "It's nothing, make it a three oh five."

Freda: When I first came on the job, I was told right off the bat that, "You can't go to Eleven Engine or Eleven Truck." I didn't even want to go there in the first place, but somebody made it their business to tell me that because my name ended in a vowel and I was Italian apparently. They said, "Because you're Italian, you're not allowed in that house." I found out later that the FMBA was a tremendous controlling factor on the fire department, much more than it is now. The FMBA would okay all transfers. Nothing transpired; no transfer was made without them and Italians were blackballed from certain houses. That's changed tremendously now. I'm sure people still have some prejudices against one race or another, but it's no where near that now. But it was strong then.

There wasn't too much racism in the fire department because there were very few blacks. In those days I didn't even know a black firefighter. I knew there was one or two, like Shelly Harris, but I didn't know them. I may not have even known who they were if I met them. So I couldn't talk about racism because the black population of the fire department was such that it didn't have to exist. But then when I went to Twelve Engine, I happened to walk in on a company that had two black firefighters. When I was promoted and got sent to this tour, I can recall people saying to me, "You know, you're going to a house that has two black firefighters in it." Trying to warn me; like I wouldn't know, I wouldn't care to go there, but I really didn't give a damn. To be honest with you, I didn't really care. I was young and I thought the world was for real. I went there and the two black firefighters who were there, I really learned to respect, like, maybe even love a lot because I really did. They were tremendous individuals.

Then I learned something about prejudice because I learned that I had a white firefighter who worked there who was an alcoholic. Now imagine me, a young fire captain with very little experience walking into the place and having an older firefighter with fifteen years' experience come up to me and say, "I don't know what you heard about me, but I cut down and I only drink seven quarts of beer a day." The man was a nice man, but he was a bum. He was dirty. He was two steps from being a derelict.

I didn't know what to do with him because he had been drinking beer for fifteen years. He started at seven-thirty in the morning and he ended up drinking all night when he went home. My point is the black firefighters were immaculate on their bodies. They both worked hard and had part time jobs. They were very respectful to me. And they were very good firefighters. You learn a lesson about people. Why would you be prejudice? How would I like one race over another? How do you stereotype people when you see that right before you, before your eyes?

Charpentier: I would say the department was ninety percent Catholic. When I came on my list was a mixture. I think off my list there were ten or twelve blacks. We had a bunch of good blacks come off that list, too, a bunch of good firemen. There were maybe ten blacks who came on before that list. But we had Italians, Irish, Germans, and a few other different groups. I think there were one or two Spanish who came on from that list. It was a mixture. I couldn't say it was fifty percent Irish or fifty percent German or anything. I would say maybe seventy or eighty percent Catholics.

I never actually had any blacks in the company when I was assigned to Six Engine, but working with them at a fire? To me I'd treated them as a person and they treated me as a person. No hard feelings, ethnic slurs, or anything. They did their share; we did our share; and if they were detailed in, they were treated like anybody else. They sat down at the table; ate with us and everything else.

It seemed way after my list came on that the attitude changed towards a lot of them. A lot of the animosity was brought about by the consent decree. They had the attitude that we're here because of the decree. You have to put so many blacks on. I think a lot of people resented it and they still resent it to this day.

Smith: I had been around men of that vent all my life. They were basically Irish, Irish-German, Italian, or Polish. The majority of them were Roman Catholic. So that didn't differ any from my friends who I grew up with. The only difference was that these men were from World War II. I was from Korea and there really wasn't that much of a gulf between us. They grew up in the early part of the Depression. I was the back end of the Depression, but we still shared a cultural identity from the Depression. To talk in a sense you might say, you walked in and you were absorbed. It was because it was homogeneous.

There were blacks who came on the job with me, but their skin color was a benign factor. Basically we all came out of the same social strata, the lower middle class. Now there was no difference between that black guy and me as far as growing up and going to school. It showed in the firehouses where these blacks were because they were included in on everything. They went to each other's house at Christmas time.

There were blacks in Twelve Engine and Five Truck. They used to come to a firehouse on detail. The guys there had their own bunks, but there were a lot of empty ones. They'd say, "Take any one you want." Nobody said, "This is for you." The color was benign. It didn't mean anything.

However, now from what I have gathered or what I have seen it becomes a mark to separate.

Dunn: In the classes in 1959 we did have black candidates come on the job and they fit in. There was no racial separation where they went to a black company or anything like that. What they did is just what I did Down Neck. Somebody says "Well, he lives on Pamona Avenue, can't we get him into Twenty-nine Engine?" I can't remember any specific racial discontent, except from what I was told prior to that where the blacks were put in the Salvage unit because they were busy and we couldn't get the white guys going into that. But that wasn't really a Newark Fire Department unit at the time. It was really just brought over to the city and regular Newark firemen didn't want the assignments either. So, they stuck some black people in there. I think Willie Thomas was one. I think Shelly Harris was one. But they developed that into a great unit and just survived. Why white people didn't want that unit, I don't know. I think it had something to do with the macho image of the fire department; that firemen put out fires and these clean-up guys come and clean up. So, you can almost put the racial context that we were using these black guys as janitorial people that clean up the fire after the big, strong firemen put out the fire.

I just didn't see any racial incidents in our class. You can certainly say at certain times, certain groups of people were assigned to certain firehouses, but I really believe it was done almost because of where you lived and what was going on. I don't know if that will ever change.

Is it cultural or racial? It's probably a combination. Nothing is black and white in these issues. If I was sitting back and I was twenty years younger, I would just take a negative to the black guy coming in because he was uncomfortable. "I don't like you either." That would be the attitude.

But fortunately for me, I went to school later on in life. I went to Essex County College, a predominantly minority school. You sit and listen to the instructors and they come from many, many backgrounds. You find that you're a little bit more open to a thought process other than what you were brought up with. As you are growing older and you start to look around, experience is a great thing. Now I see people who are uncomfortable or come up with a problem. They say, "You know, I'm uncomfortable." I try to give it a little more thought as to what's going on. Why is this happening?

I always remember what one specific black guy said to me one time. I asked him why doesn't he sit down with us and have dinner. I know you have your little brown bag. He said "I just don't feel comfortable." From that conversation we went into the whole thing of where he was brought up. How he didn't have a family. He was living in a foster home. He lived in a totally black community. Nowhere in his schooling did anybody ever bring up the fact that you're just as good as everybody else. You know, you don't have to stay in the corner. Basically that's what he was doing in the firehouse. He wound up in deep trouble because he was a disciplinary problem in the fire department with drugs in a short time. He just went on and continued what he was brought up in his cultural way and he wound up dead.

You ask, "Did the fire department have anything to do with that?" No. From the day he was born, he was born into a system. Maybe if we could allude to that in our training somewhere in the system, as young people come on, that this is a microcosm of society. There are all different people here. We have people preaching Islam in the fire department. I don't know anything about Islam, but I still respect your religion. Other people seem to be like, "Well, we're not quite that open." You're a Catholic; it's not good to talk to them too much because you don't know what they're up to. What I was told as a young kid about the Orange men in Ireland, I see happening on the fire department. Most of the people don't want to get involved in religion, economics, or culture. They really don't. They want everything to match them. That's not happening, but I don't know if there's any real solution to that because it's an on-going thing.

There have always been numerous religions discussed. Anything other than what I do, I really don't care too much about. What I've learned from the schooling is that, I give everybody the respect I think they're entitled to. It's funny when you watch some of these things transpire. Something that should be addressed in the fire service, that's probably going to have to be in time, is that the dictates of certain religions interfere in fire department functions. Some people take affront to a black man who wants to pray at two o'clock in the afternoon. You turn towards Mecca and you say your prayers. Can you do it privately? Should you do it on the apparatus floor? I don't know, but it wouldn't bother me. I would probably walk away from the incident more than try to aggravate the guy by saying, "Would you stop making that noise? I'm trying to sleep."

I would try to give the man that type of courtesy. All our people are certainly not doing that. It shows up in odd things, like our holidays with overtime. You'll see who will work. You can almost pick out the race of the man by who's working on what day. So you say, "Wow, so there is a reflection here." But if you see a day with all the white guys working and there are no blacks we don't think about why no blacks are working that day. It isn't our culture, so we don't know about it. We're not very broadminded in our reaching out because we want to stay within our culture. I guess that's very normal for us to do that. So, there is a problem there, but answers?

Carragher: I have heard stories that if you weren't Irish, you couldn't get into Central Avenue. That's true. That's what I was told. I never found that problem, but I was told the same thing. A few years before '59, you couldn't get into Six Engine unless you were German. You had to be a German to get into Six Engine. Chief Zoppi, Joe Zoppi was a Battalion Chief in the Third Battalion. He was one of the first Italians on the job and he was harassed quite severely as a captain in Five Truck. That's going back I would say probably in the '40s, late '40s, early '50s because he came on the job prior to World War II.

Harris: Joe Denardo and I were both assigned to Engine Company Twelve at the time. It was interesting because when we went there they said, "Okay, go up there. The tour you're going to be working on, they're working right now. So, go introduce yourself." So, that's what we did.

We walked in and they were eating and I remember they had a big pot of hot dogs and beans. Everybody is sitting around eating. When I walked in, there was one guy I knew, Kenny Gibson and only because Kenny lived a block away from me in North Newark at the time. We weren't friends, but I knew Kenny Gibson and his brother Hooter. We went in. They offered us something to eat. Then what they did was the captain who was going to be in Engine Company Twelve, he took Joe and said, "Come on, you don't have the gear, but I'm going to give you some gear. Try this on." Do this and everything. My captain never said a word, never offered me anything.

We came to work. Reggie Evelyn had old stuff and he said, "Come here kid. You use this." But my captain never offered me anything or showed me anything. Then the next interesting part was when we went upstairs. Joe's captain said, "Pick out any bed you want." My captain took me upstairs and said, "If nobody is sleeping in those beds when we work, you guys have those three beds." I said, "What do you mean those three beds?" Blacks were only assigned certain beds. Even in Twelve Engine, there were three beds. Those were the only three beds blacks would sleep in. Whites had eight bunks on that side. They can pick and choose and there were two in the middle that they can choose to sleep in. We had three bunks in the corner and that was it.

On the second tour there were three blacks. On the fourth tour there were two. On the third tour there was Cliff Evelyn, Charlie Chapman, and one other guy. And on the first tour it was Ben Joseph and Bill Jackson. So, there were enough bunks for the guys and that's where you had to sleep. The other thing was you were told there were certain things you couldn't use. In this day and age, when I came on this job in 1961, they had segregated beds. Then there were certain things in the firehouse, the blacks couldn't touch. That belonged to the other guys, the white guys, the Caucasians in the fire department, things like different cups, eating utensils. Bucky Evelyn said, "Come here. This is what you do. This is what you can use. This is what you do." And he explained to me the system of what you do.

There were blacks in Twelve Engine, Seventeen Engine, Twenty-nine Engine, Five Truck, and Salvage Two. Those were the houses, oh and Eleven Engine, those were the houses we were able to work in when we were assigned to work. When I came on the job there were two guys in Eleven Engine. It remained that way for a long time. The majority stayed in Twelve Engine, Seventeen, and Twenty-nine.

Rocky Highsmith went to Nineteen Engine. Oh, there was an uproar. Nobody wanted this black guy to come to Nineteen Engine. Gerry was down there maybe a tour, maybe two. I get a phone call. "You so and so, so and so." "What is your problem?" "Why did you make me go down here? These guys don't want me down here." I say, "Gerry, just stay there for a while." John Kossup worked in the Post Office. Gerry worked in the Post Office and John got Gerry to take the job. So, he calls up and cusses John out. John says, "I didn't do it."

All the guys who were working at Nineteen Engine were on the Newark Fire Department softball team. I would say a good eighty percent of the guys who were on that team worked in that house. Less than a month after Gerry's on the job, they found out Gerry can play ball. Played football, played baseball, he was good. Now they embrace him. You're our buddy. Gerry played with them and Bob Griffith. You know, the operator, he was the pitcher on their team, one of the best in the country. They went to the international softball league up in Canada and won it. They'll all tell you to this day, because Gerry came and played the shortstop and everything for them, they were now able to do this.

I went out for that raggedy team and they told me I couldn't make the team. And I was playing against Bob. I was playing against Gerry in other leagues, the Industrial League, the Board of Education League. I was playing against these guys all the time. But I couldn't make the fire department team. At that time I was saying, "Them racist bastards just don't want me on the team." Then Gerry went down there. He has the type of temperament that lets him sit in and fit in; everything started working out from there.

The other thing about the job that used to make me angry was promotional exams. I stopped taking promotional exams when guys in a study class that a chief was giving came out from number one to fifteen on a list. Three other guys, dropped off to like nineteen, twenty, and twenty-one because they forgot some questions. They changed the whole exam about two weeks before we took it. There were like fifty questions on the rulebook. Who reads the rulebook? You got it when you first came on. You may have paid attention to it for your first couple of months and then you threw it in the locker and that was the end of it. You probably never saw it again. And there was first-aid on that exam. Everybody's studying the hydraulics, the formulas and building construction. I said, "What the hell is the sense of taking an exam?" And I stopped taking exams.

The other thing about taking exams which used to aggravate me was if they gave an exam in Newark, maybe the next month they gave it in Passaic or Paterson or Camden. You could get into your car and come to Newark because everybody came out and wrote down questions and you had almost the exam. And they gave practically the same exam everywhere at that time. But if I came to you and asked you for, "Hey, you had the exam. What can you give me?" Oh, no, no, no. You might be a friend, but if he gave you something he was now ostracized. He couldn't be a part of that establishment anymore because he gave the blacks or Hispanics something. And that's the problem we had. I said, "This isn't fair. This is totally unfair to have to do this."

Then the other thing that made all blacks angry on the job was it was usually a two year list. If we came out on that list and were anywhere in that top fifteen, the list would stop at ten. In that two year period they usually get about twenty captains. Then they got messed up because we had Meryl King and Bucky Evelyn come in like number four, number five. Now to get the rest of their people they have to promote these guys, but prior to that if you came anywhere over fifteen, the list stopped. And they wouldn't promote.

Ernie Smith was the first one to file a lawsuit against the City of Newark for doing that. He lost, but he was the first one to do that. We went to Mayor Gibson first. Judge William Walls was then the Corporation

Counsel for the City of Newark. We sat with the Mayor, Ernie Smith, myself, Minatee, I think Thomas. We even had a white guy, an Italian guy, Mike Mieli. Mike's a Lieutenant up in the county now. He left the job. He even came down with us to complain about racism in the fire department, promotions and stuff because he had taken the exam a couple of times and they didn't promote him. He worked out of Twelve Engine also on the fourth tour.

We sat with them for a good, maybe two hours. We had stuff stacked up to document different guys not getting on the job, guys not being promoted, how they stopped the list, guys being knocked off the job for petty junk. We waited about five months. We kept calling the Mayor. We kept calling the Corporation Counsel. They wouldn't talk to us anymore and we worked hard for Gibson to win, but now all of the sudden, he isn't talking to us. We went back to him. Finally, he gave us an answer. He said, "Well, I can't do anything with this." Okay, fine.

So we decide we're going to file a law suit for promotions and entrance. When we did this I had to sign because at that time I was the president of the Vulcans, so my name went on the paper. We went into court, after it finally got into court, and we had a lawyer, a black lawyer, who was doing them a favor working for stuff. We were feeding him and he was doing what he had to do, filing a claim in court and everything. We went into court. The first person that they called to testify was Mayor Gibson. The first thing that came out of his mouth was, "There has never been discrimination in the Newark Fire Department or any employee in the City of Newark. If they pass the exam they will be promoted or they could have been promoted."

So, we're saying, "What are you talking about? We gave you this stuff and proved it to you." And that's what he said on the stand. The judge basically said, "Get out of here." That was the end of that case. We said, "Okay." We went back to Judge Wall, talked to him again. A year later we got the other departments, guys who made up the Vulcan Pioneers, which was strictly a social club at the time, we got them to come in with us. There are thirteen towns. We asked them would they go in on the lawsuit with us, thinking that if we did it together, we might have more of a chance.

We didn't have any money. We were able to scrounge and do little things to get in. We were able to do this, but now we don't have any money. How are we going to do this? Then somebody calls us to say, "Go over to Rutgers." So what is it? Rutgers University Law Clinic, Professor Highman, he's in charge. We go to see him. We sit down. We explain what we want to do. And his eyes lit up. "This sounds beautiful. I'm taking this case."

He has his senior law students doing all the paper work. Doing all the things, going to the library, doing whatever they have to do. We go back into court. About seven months down the road we're back in the court. We get beat again. The judge throws it out, the judge that's still handling the case, Judge Politan. Twice now he's thrown out our case. So, now here we go again. We don't have a dime. We keep going back to the clinic and they're rehashing what we did. Maybe if we try this, we'll do this, we'll do this.

A lady I knew from the Salvation Army says, "I've got a good lawyer for you." "Who?" She gives me this female lawyer. I call her up. We talk to her. She says, "I want to make a name for myself, establish myself in Newark and around New Jersey. I'll take your case." So, we hooked her up with Highman. They got the case. They got together. This time we go into court and that's how the decree was won. That's how we won that decree. But three times we got kicked in the butt. Judge Politan threw it out.

The first time we blamed on Gibson. The second time we didn't do our homework, but then the third time we went in, this lady and Highman and the Rutgers Law Clinic they put together that case and it was beautiful and that's how we got the decree put in. What we asked them to do when we went down and we testified down in the State was give us ten books to study and say the exam will come out of those ten books. Now if I study those ten books and I fail, that's my fault. That's what we asked them to do. That's the only thing. And we had more fights with people about that. "Why should they tell you that?" Why not? Make it a level playing field. A lot of guys would say, "You're a trouble maker." Fine, I'm a trouble maker, but I'm only doing what I think you would do if something was going against you in a situation like that.

Before that decree was basically implemented here in the State of New Jersey, the Atlanta, Georgia Police Department and the Georgia highway patrolman came up here. They had heard about it. They sat with Highman and everything with their attorney. They got what they did, took it back down south. They were able to integrate and have promotions and things in their department twice as fast as us and we're the ones who first went into court and did that on a federal level. And they were able to do it. They did it in three places, Seattle, Bridgeport, and Hartford, Connecticut. Within five years of that suit Hartford had the first black Director of a fire department. I think to this day, that will be one of the things I'll remember most, going and doing that.

It was able, to me I believe, bring more blacks, Hispanics into the job, not only in the city of Newark, but throughout the state and other places throughout the country. They came in, used our stuff and were able to be successful with it. It's so funny, if you go to places like East Orange, Jersey City, and Camden and if you see the makeup of the department you'll see this law suit has helped them tremendously. East Orange I'd say is ninety per cent minority now.

But you look at the city of Newark, five years ago, we went back into court because we felt like for every five Caucasians that were being put on the job, only one minority was still being put on, even though we had won this law suit. The city of Newark now has a black Mayor. The city Council is three quarters black, one Hispanic, and one Italian. They have not been submitting the records and everything to the Federal Judge. And the Judge brought them back in and said, "What is wrong with you people. If you don't start doing it again, we're going to fine you."

But you realize how long ago? Up until five years ago we had to come back in and fight with these people. Everybody else has made gains by it but the city of Newark. Well, we have made gains to the point where we have numerous officers now, which we never had before. The Chief of the department is black and we had a black Director. All of this was because of the different things we as an organization did. We stopped being a social organization and started fighting. It almost changed around again. By that I mean is this, the young blacks in the job and the Hispanics, they look at us as old fossils, seriously. They say to us, "You didn't help me get no job. I did this." Yes, you took the exam, but we did fight for you so you had these steps you didn't have to go through.

There have been situations in the Newark Fire Department since then. They're hanging up signs and stuff like Sambo on the wall and saying this is that. And the guys don't say anything about this. You are supposed to take it upon yourself now and fight these things. You don't let them go on. I'm not saying you need to have a hundred per cent of this, but what I'm saying is we need to stand up for what we fought for and you need to carry it on. But they don't get it. The young blacks are making a good dollar.

I think John P. Caufield messed up. When we had that first exam after we won the lawsuit, I personally knocked down, ten blacks, two Hispanics, and three whites. I had every black guy on this job mad at me. But I said, "I don't want them on the job for one reason. When we did the investigation they were thieves, drug addicts, dealers and users, one guy we had was a murderer. We don't want these guys on the job." And I said, "The reason Caufield is going to allow them to come on the job is so he looks good when he makes his report. We let them on the job and see what kind of guys we got."

Out of all those guys they let back on the job, only one of them is still on this job today. They were all fired, all fired eventually. We've made a lot of strides and I think we'll continue to do so, but the guys on the job will have to take it upon themselves to stand up. If something happens, learn to stand up and be counted.

But I think Newark would have reached the consent decree goals if the department hadn't lost so many people. In this day and age with the changes in the administration after Gibson left and with the Council changing the way it did, I think it would have changed it. I think they would have reached it, but it's just impossible to reach because nobody is being put on.

Highsmith: The first time I really threw a racist at somebody, was for my own benefit. We were at Nineteen Engine and Captain Minor was our captain. It was Owen Donnelly, myself, Freddie Scalera, and Jimmy Conlon. We were the crew. Lady was on her way to the airport and she ran out of gas in the gas station across the street from us. Okay, we went over there, saw what the problem was. She said, "I'm due at the airport and I've got a plane to catch and I ran out of gas." So in the firehouse we used to have about a five to ten gallon gas can because we'd fill up the engines. If it didn't come to ten gallons or if it came thirteen gallons, we'd put two gallons there, make it fifteen, round figure, just to have it on hand. We took the gas across the street; put it in this lady's tank; and sent her on her way. Next night we're all sitting out front, nice balmy night. Car conks out across the street at Weequahic Park. Go across the street. See what the problem was. They happened to be black. "I don't know. My car just stopped." So, Owen said, "Come on." We went back across the street.

Each firehouse had a battery charger. We're half way across the street with the battery charger. I heard someone whistle and then say, "Hey, kiddo. Hey kiddo." I looked around. It's Captain Minor. I said, "Yes, sir Captain." He said, "Come here. You can't use fire department stuff for that. You can't use fire department stuff for civilians." I said, "Yes, sir Captain. I'll be right back." Owen and I went across the street; gave the man a jump start; and came back.

He said, "I'm going to call the chief." I said, "Let me tell you something, Cap." I said, "Yesterday, a white lady stopped across the street in the gas station. We gave her gas. You didn't say anything. Today, a black guy comes over there. He gets stuck. We give him a jump. You jump in on me. Chief Iannuzzi came down here and said, 'Nobody can be in the racks during the day until after two p.m. The guys go upstairs to sleep. You don't say anything. I went upstairs to sleep. You came up there to wake me up. Do you have a racial problem or something?" He said, "I don't have to take that. I'm going to call the Chief." I said, "Before you call the Chief, Captain, sit down, because I'm going to get it all off my back."

I start telling him things that came up to me that I thought might have been racist on his part or prejudice on his part, not racist, prejudice because he was always a decent guy. He sat down there for a minute. He thought. I walked away. I used a few spicy words in there you know because the street came out in me there. I was man, not fireman. I was a man then and I was angry. He sat down and he looked at me. Next night, come to work five o'clock. Said, "Hi, Cap." "Hi, kiddo." No more problems. Not another word said about it.

But being in the department now, having to deal with people it's just a shame. It's bad with all the animosity going on between whites and blacks. I thought we were over that. But you know that it's still going on. That's another thing I can't understand. Hey, we sleep just about in the same bed. Why are you going to be angry with me? Why should we be angry with each other? Outside world is something different, but when we're here together, it shouldn't be like that. That's how I thought.

Cody: At Six Engine, Chief Donlan and John Ryan and the men of the company had a feud going. So, I wanted to go to Six Engine. I thought that was the best place to be. I really wanted to be busy. I got that spot in Six Engine on the third tour not knowing that no one else wanted it. I ended up there and I'm happy as can be. Then I realize what the problems are. That there was nothing that the men could do or I could do that would please Chief Donlan. He used to come into my room, sometimes at three o'clock in the afternoon and inform me that the windows weren't washed or that the pole wasn't polished. It was just nit picking after nit picking after nit picking, to the point where Chief Donlan had to call the Battalion Chief to call me because I couldn't take it anymore. "You're not my supervisor. Talk to my Battalion Chief." It was driving the Battalion Chief crazy. Finally I called the union and just put in for any spot, anywhere, any tour.

That's how bad I wanted to get out of there because it just wasn't fun going to work.

As far as the consent decree is concerned, I believe there would have been a change without it. It would have come about anyway, but not as quickly. When you start blocking out a certain group of people and giving higher weights to other people, it's going to happen faster.

The whole consent decree thing has had an effect on morale. There was some real animosity between groups of firefighters at one time. I mean you come out on the captain's list. You're number four or five on the captain's list and they throw this list out and have another test which was more or less like a lottery system. The guy next to you comes out number four and you come out number fifty-three. You're going to have animosity. You're going to have a problem, especially if this guy becomes your boss. They've made people that don't belong as officers. And yet they come in and start flexing their muscles with guys who had studied and had been passed over, you're just going to have a problem. But I think we've been using this system for so long that anyone who was passed over on the other list was made off another one.

I've never seen a racial problem on the department. I've never seen it. You might have certain individuals who might have had a racial problem, but I've never seen anything where blacks were against whites or whites were against blacks. I don't see those things. I realize they happen and they probably are happening, but I have this pie in the sky attitude, like everything is fine, because I'm happy. If you surround yourself in the fire department with the right guys, you're happy.

Garrity: When I first went to Avon Avenue, there were no minorities in the firehouse. Shortly thereafter, there were some who came in and there were some tensions. It never manifested itself into anything violent, but you knew when this guy came into relieve you or you were there to relieve him there was no conversation. There was no sitting around the table bullshitting at relief time. The guy, if he came in to relieve us, the guy he was relieving just left. If the guy came in to relieve him, he left. So there was that tension, but after about a year it went away, because don't forget we had some real bull nuts up there. When I left it wasn't like that anymore.

But ethnic and minority tensions on the job haven't gone away. I'm talking about those incidents that I dealt with. I'm sure there are more tensions in different areas now than there were before because there are more minorities. It just doesn't work sometimes. I got along with people because of them not because of the racial anything, but some guys can't do that. You can go out into the field now and find guys who have been on the job two years and can't stand anybody whether you're white or black, it doesn't make any difference to them. And there are other guys who it doesn't bother.

Nine Truck is a perfect example, the first tour up there. You have two guys up there who have been there for a long time and two black guys and they get along fine. The thing that I found is the guys work and they intermingle with the group. Before they moved Eighteen Engine out of there and they had twelve people there they would eat dinner with us and do all that kind of stuff that you normally do. That was something that I insisted on. I sort of moved them to eat dinner with us because when you sit down and eat dinner it makes things a lot easier. When guys sit around the table and eat dinner, things change. You're a little leery of them and now he's sitting down to eat with you and he's cleaning the pots.

When Al Taylor moved, we helped him move. He had a party, we went to his party, our wives, everybody. As far as that house at that time there was no problem. Now, I was up there the other night. Al was off, but Courtney was there. Courtney's very quiet. So originally they thought he didn't like anybody. It's just that he's quiet. He's not like the rest of us, loud and screaming and ranting and raving. He's just not that way, but he fits into the program now. So in that instance in that particular place there were no problems on that tour. Originally yes, then it went away. I was up there the other night and I didn't see any.

Any tension didn't go to the fire ground. Not in our company. There were instances that it did go to the fire ground with someone who worked with us and a guy in another company. I'm not going to mention any names, but this particular guy didn't like any blacks. We had a three bagger on Bergen Street. The guy who worked for me did something that this guy didn't like and there was a fist fight on the landing between the second and the third floor. It was just because of racial things.

Prachar: There have been racial tensions between firefighters. I've been in spots where white didn't talk to black and vise a versa. Some guys feeling they're better than the others. Some guys just out and out don't like them. Both ways, black guy doesn't like the white guy. The white guy doesn't like the black guy. Especially now with all this stuff with the captains' test, very bitter towards the majority, not all of them, but towards the majority of black. And not all the blacks dislike the white guys. There are guys out there I'll talk to as black guys. There are some out there I won't treat with respect because that's the way I feel about them. I'm not a hard guy to get along with. If you can't get along with me, then there's a problem. Therefore I'll treat you the way I think you should be treated. Not only racially between white and black or Hispanic, I'll do that to a white guy too.

But a lot of the black guys out there feel they've been mistreated for two hundred years. There are some who don't go along that line and don't want to be treated that way. They want to earn it the way it should be earned, not given. That's why you have the problem as far as racial. Because some of them feel you should give it to me. My theory is you show me a two hundred year old black and I'll show you somebody who deserves it, but these young kids here they should go out and work for their money.

The younger generation takes it for granted because now they expect it. I'm not going to work for this because I could sue and get it. So why should I work when I could have it handed to me. As compared to some of them who would say, "I'd just as soon work." Now some of them you can joke around with using black and white and everything. Some of them you don't dare because they'll have you up on a board or something for discrimination of some type, racial slurs or something. You have to know where to talk and where not to talk with some of these people. It doesn't matter black or white, I'm saying with all sides.

There are some guys out there that I could talk to that other people can't. There are a couple of them out there, black guy for instance, that I'll call him racial slurs to his face, but don't you do it because you're not accepted by him where I am because it's all how you treat the person. If I'm treated good; I'll treat you good and vise a versa. And the one guy I'm talking about now there's probably ninety percent of the guys who work in and around him, who hate the guy's guts because he's black. But I treat him for what he is and I can talk to the man.

The man was more or less bounced out of another company because they felt he was a chicken and he can't fight fires. I've been in two situations with the man where it was just me and him, black and white, side by side. Anybody says anything about the guy; I'll go against that person before I'll go against this guy. Because I've been there, I've worked with the guy. Maybe the guy's improved since he's been on the job, but to this day I'll walk hand in hand with the guy. I would go into a fire with him and not be afraid. Where some other guys, I would hesitate and hold back some. Not this guy. Not a lot of the black guys who I worked with. Seventeen Engine, fourth tour, you couldn't find a better crew. When it comes time to fighting a fire a lot of it stops, but when you come out it's right there again. We have to do what we have to do, but when we're finished doing what we're doing then it's over with.

The Federal Government getting involved in the department was the biggest problem. If they would have let things go the way they were going with a proper test, everything would be fine. It's just a handful of people who came in and wanted, wanted, wanted, but didn't want to work for it that destroyed the whole situation. And that's where it sits right now. It was a handful that grew bigger. And now some of them are starting to look and say "Hey, maybe this shouldn't be." I know guys who don't want to be in the organization. I know guys who aren't in the organization and couldn't care less about that organization.

The people in that organization feel they helped, but in the long run they've hurt because that's where all your racial tensions come from. There might have been guys who where good friends, but because of this don't even talk anymore. Because it was a forced move by a small number of people and it was forced on everybody, even the ones who didn't belong. Guys who didn't belong to that organization are still the bad guys. Because even though you don't belong to it, you may benefit from it, but it's hurting you, tension wise, out in the field.

It started out as a social club. Sure, they needed their social club. Just like the Irish need their Irish clubs. The Italians have your Italian clubs.

There was the Holy Name Society. Everybody had their own organization, but you didn't see the Irish come in and demand this. You didn't see the Italians come in and demand that. Just one group came in and said, "We want, we want." And they got. Everybody had their clubs, if everybody else did, why not. It's just a matter of where they took their club beyond being a club.

It's going to take the department a long time to get over the polarization because most of the people that it affected just came on this job and will never forget. It may not affect the guys in the most recent classes, but it has affected the guys in front of them. Guys with five years have gone through all this torture. Seeing what happened to all their friends. What it did to them. What it did to their family life and everything, I'll never forget it. The only way the guys in the recent classes would be affected is if they're in the house with hatred because of all this, then it will come down the hill. But it will take a long time for this to turn around.

Finucan: We had problems with the other crews working with us. There's no question about it. There was absolute racism in those days. I was really shocked because it was my first experience of ever dealing with blacks on the job, intimately as a captain in an engine company with the older guys. What I had found out was I had four excellent people. They had families. They each had their own idiosyncrasies, just like any individual does, but I had the good fortune to know them as individuals and not as blacks.

I never considered myself to be a bleeding heart liberal. Not now, not ever and I would have to say this was a very, very racist fire department in those days, very racist. A lot of otherwise good firemen, good people, when they became part of a group, they just behaved in very strange ways towards an individual. You would know a person one way on a one to one basis, but the minute he was put with his group, his engine company, or his peers, fellow WASPs, it was like a total night and day. Although I have no firsthand knowledge because of the way things went. There was a lot of innuendo. There were a lot of things that were said that I knew for a fact weren't true and yet they were still said.

We were a very racist fire department in those days. And the racism for the most part wasn't outright. Mainly, because I think anybody who knows me knows that if it was I would be right on it. I would put them on charges. I mean I'm not the type of guy who is going to punch somebody in the nose, but I would definitely be putting people on charges. Never had to do that because I was always up front in the way I ran a company. People knew me and I guess they knew what to expect from me. But I always thought the racism was very insidious. That it was just an underlying thing all over. From the help you get at fires, from picking up your own hose, and a lot of stuff that wasn't there. I saw all sides of it. I came from all sides. With my varied career on the job, I've seen both sides. And I know the camaraderie of engine companies who work together. It's a good thing. It's a nice thing to have. And I can also tell you when it's missing and when it's lacking. I've seen both and I can tell you with the black crew that there was nothing there. So, I would have to somehow figure racism had something to do with it.

It would spill on to the fire ground insidiously, not always up front, but a lot of times it was up front. We had a lot of real hard heads on Belmont Avenue. We had certain individuals, rough and tumble guys who were writing racial slurs on the walls and pasting cartoons and various things, pranks and stuff like that in Twelve Engine. We put up with that for all the years I was there, but those guys were just knuckleheads. It was always very underhanded and it was the typical type of racism that blacks are constantly harping about that happens.

This is my experience with my engine company on the Newark Fire Department. I'm not saying that it happens all over the world or it's in every case, but in my case. I hate to have to agree with people who say there is racism out there. But in my experience I have to say it was true. It was absolutely true in my case. That's what I think. Now, I know my own personality and sometimes I think maybe it was just me that they were after or that they disliked for whatever reasons. So, there is a shadow of a doubt in my mind because after all I was the captain of the company. I often thought that if there was some very popular captain running that company whether that group would have been able to meld into the system more. But with me there we never did. So, I am never sure to this day and I will never be sure whether or not it was me or them or a combination of both. If I had to make some sort of a judgment I would say it was eighty percent because they were black and that's the total racism and twenty percent because I am not the type of guy who would be able to overcome that type of problem.

There are captains who can. If Frank Calvetti was the captain at Twelve Engine he probably would have been able to help that company fit in under extremely adverse conditions, the built in racism. I'm not saying Calvetti could do it, but I'm giving you an example of the type guy it would take. A guy like Calvetti may have been able to make that company fit in, into a white fire department better than I did. But I'm not making any excuses. I always do the job the best I can and that's the best I could do at the time. That was one of the areas that I felt that I was probably not that successful at. I never let it worry me and I just carried on. I never transferred out of that company. I stayed there until I got promoted. I wouldn't have left that company. So much for the racism end of it, it was definitely there. It's a sorry, shameful thing, but it was there.

I don't know if it's improved. I'm less in contact with what's going on out there. I don't know. I think maybe in the last years or two it has. In the last year or two or three years it might have, but I really can't say for sure. I hope it's getting better out there. I hope it's not getting worse. But I think it might be getting better.

Cosby: When I went to Eighteen Engine they told me I was the first black firefighter assigned there. I didn't have that many problems there. Naturally you always hear racial remarks, but not only against black guys. You hear them against white guys too. You always hear racial remarks concerning Polish, Italians. I think the only kind of remarks I didn't hear were against Anglo-Saxon Protestants. I guess nobody had anything to say about them. But basically it wasn't that bad because we had a chief. I was in the house with Chief Donlon. He was the Deputy Chief at that time assigned to Eighteen. He was pretty strict. He wouldn't let them get away with anything in his company.

On the fire department as a whole, I would say I was accepted. I would say blacks were accepted pretty well at that time. Compared to stories I'd heard when the first guys came on. There really weren't that many blacks on the job even when I came on. There was only maybe probably about thirty-five or forty. One problem was the social settings in the fire department. A lot of times you would have a fear of being isolated because you were more or less the only black in the firehouse. A lot of times you would find yourself in situations where you wouldn't have that much in common with a lot of the fellows, they being from different backgrounds or whatever. But I feel like I always had to do a job really, not to basically socialize.

When I transferred to Central Avenue, I didn't find any blatant racism. I was more or less accepted. On my tour there were two Italian guys, myself, one German. I suppose the rest were Irish. On the first tour, I think they were all Irish. Captain Melody was the captain at the time. Everybody on his tour, I think, was Irish. On the fourth tour there were at least two black guys Hank Bullock and Henry Carr. If I'm not mistaken Julius Banks was there, but he later transferred out. But I never had too many problems with the guys, just one incident. One incident I had over there. There was a time when black firefighters had pulled out of the union because the union wouldn't support affirmative action. The guys on my tour became angry at me for pulling out of the union. They had made threats against me.

I just wrote a report on it, sent a report in to the Director. From that time on I didn't have any more problems because the report was hanging over their heads. At that time affirmative action was being pushed by the government. I think it was beginning to have an effect on the Newark Fire Department. A lot of white guys, I know, resented that. There were a lot of threats and stuff. I think that added to this problem that is still prevalent today. That divided the black and white firefighters even more, the question of affirmative action.

I can see affirmative action because blacks had been denied access to the fire department for years. When you come to the point where the second black firefighter appointed to the job is still on the job. That's telling you something. I don't think anybody could even tell you the second white firefighter on the job. Nobody could even remember. But I can actually remember the first black firefighter and the second black firefighter who is Shelly Harris. He's still on the job. The first black firefighter, Bill Thomas,

I don't think it's been ten years since he died. When you can remember things like that, that shows you how far we are behind. If we keep depending on the pace we're going now. I don't know. We'll catch up in two hundred years.

But what kind of bothers me about people who oppose affirmative action and so called quotas, is it never seemed to bother them how they have dealt with other countries. After World War II, they completely rebuilt the country of Japan. Japan was helped, Germany was helped and black people in this country ask for a little help and it's just a big uproar. You take a country like Japan, which has been helped by the United States. The perception is now that Japanese cars are better than American cars and we're buying their cars more than American cars. So what does the auto industry call for, they call for a quota on Japanese imports. Why are they doing this? Because they need a helping hand, they need help. So I think the same situation applies to blacks, where we need help. We are behind, maybe educationally and whatever. Still, if they can call for quotas on automobiles to help the automobile industry out, what's wrong with calling for quotas to help us?

I don't think we suffer in this country because we're black, it's because we're not the majority. People are basically going to take care of their own. If most of the jobs are controlled by whites in this country and we more or less have to get a job through them. What they're going to do if they're going to hire somebody, they're going to hire their relatives first. If they can't get any relatives to do the job, then they're going to go to their own people. They're going to hire someone white. That's the way it is. You're going to hire your friends. I put it this way. Your relatives come first, friends second. Most white people have white friends and most white people have white relatives. That's the way I look at it. Discrimination obviously, it's not intentional, but you can't help but have discrimination because of that concept. One race is in control, so what they're going to do is they're going to hire their relatives first, then their friends. That's what happens. I think everybody suffers to a certain extent under that.

If someone is Irish most likely most of his relatives will be Irish and it goes on down the line. Based on that, I don't think there's a way we can make progress in the fire department or in the country unless there is some kind of affirmative action. There has to be something to make some progress. The way the country is going. The way it is, you're always creating an underclass of people. The country is not going to survive. I remember I heard a Southern Senator say one time, they had the press interviewing him about the things he did towards racism and relations and stuff. He was down in Mississippi. He said, "I know there's discrimination in Mississippi. I know the things I do are wrong, but that's what the people want." He said, "I know that eventually the country is going to go under if this continues." So, he said, "Well, so be it. That's what the people want." I have two grandchildren and I would hate to see them go through a lot of things I had to go through. I always hoped this would be a better world and country.

McDonnell: I don't think the Consent Decree was necessary. It was a lie. The Justice Department evidently came to them. But without them saying the test was racist and there was discrimination, without them signing and being the complainants this could have never happened. They used to seek them out. It was Rutgers Law School that did it. I had done the Police exam. When I came on this job, I took both tests at the same time and I was on both lists. I didn't take the police job. I got letters for years from Rutgers Law School saying you may have been the victim of discrimination.

Because I had an Anglo-Saxon name; I lived in Newark; and they thought I was black or I might be black. They went out and recruited people and they made that phony charge. There was no racism involved.

There's racism now. That's the whole purpose of affirmative action. It's racism, a racist policy. It was a joke because if you go back and look at what blacks said previous to the 70's, it was civil service was their only fair chance to get a job. What happened really was that, starting in the late '60s, early '70s blacks started getting elected as mayors of cities in the country. They realized quickly that civil service was preventing them from handing these jobs out. They couldn't just give the job out to who they wanted because of civil service. Even white politicians at the time civil service was instituted always wanted to get rid of it because they can't use the jobs for patronage. So they were all happy to go along with it. Affirmative action was a way to destroy the civil service merit system. That's basically what they did. They didn't get what they really wanted where they could pick and choose whoever they want. What they did in effect was destroy the merit system because they changed their exams from objectively scored exams to subjectively scored exams, so that they could maneuver. The other way you had to know the answer. It didn't matter what color you were. It wasn't discriminatory. This is the racism now, today.

Without the Vulcans making that charge there never would have been any consent decree. It was just a lie. The Justice Department and Rutgers Law School over there, appealed to their racism. At that time they had started the Vulcan Pioneers and I think they thought they were going to take over and become the majority on the job. Those guys were going to be the head of the union or something. Their organization would be like the union. They would run the union. It hasn't worked out for them the way it was supposed to work out for them. They've done away with just about everything, every qualification for the job, but still you have to work at it.

The blacks do recruit their own and the whites recruit the whites. But what I think happens is the guys who really wanted the job came and worked out. I worked on the training, the mandatory training that you have to have now. It doesn't matter whether you're white or black. If you looked at who's on the list, it's the guys who came every day. They came and worked their brains out and that's it.

They're not recruiting people who they should be recruiting. You got some guy who has no interest in the job. We'll get 18,000 people to take the test. That's for the percentage stuff. Any statistical anomaly that we can come up with shows racism. You're going to hire 80 people? You're going to test 18,000? It was ludicrous. What they've done was they destroyed the whole system. A system that was good for the people of this country. That served them for a hundred years and they destroyed it. It's who wants the job. The kid who came there every night was the kid appointed. I heard that even before I worked in it. Before I got involved with the training, I had a black guy tell me one time, "The people you see on this job, those are the people I saw at the training." That's what it is. Plus you have white guys who want to be on the job. They want to be firemen. They don't like that. I mean what the hell. What difference does it make? The guy wants to be a fireman. That's the whole, supposedly, that's the whole idea. The guy wants to be a fireman, it not supposed to matter what color he is. It does matter to them. It matters to the people in the federal government.

There's a division on the department. Some of it was there all along, but it certainly got aggravated and exacerbated by the consent decree, definitely. Because everybody knows it's a bullshit story, white and black. Whether they'll admit it or not, say it publicly. Privately they'll say it. The white guys and the black guys got along at least. They may not have fraternized together, but it's a two way street. It's always white people who are racists. I grew up in the projects. I was the white kid in the black neighborhood. I was the white kid in the gym with fifty black kids, so I know it's a two way street. I would go to play football with the white kids; it was the blacks who were the niggers. When I was in the gym playing basketball with the black guys it was the honkies and all that, so it was a two way street. I heard both sides. I think the white guys and the black guys, previous to the consent decree, at least got along. They got along. They probably didn't hang out too much together or whatever, but I don't think there was the animosity toward each other that came after the consent decree. Because people feel like they're getting screwed. It's not really a fair shot.

I think the animosity is pretty wide spread, but it's an individual thing. Guys get along. It's true anywhere there's prejudice like that. The guy you know is okay, but the other guy isn't. The black guy you work with is all right. The white guy you work with, well he's not a bad guy, but the other white guy who I don't know is a piece of shit. There's a lot of resentment that is unspoken and that you only hear in your own racial group. There's a lot of it. And a lot of it is justified.

They took something that was really good, that was a fair system and that served the city and the people and the men and this job well. The people of this city had a great fire department. The firemen could trust the guy who they worked with. You need that morale, that trust, that spirit in a job like this. You can't pay people to risk their lives. You have to know that when you go in that building, that guy can be trusted. My life is in his hands. People don't feel that way today. They can't trust that guy. I was a fireman with George Daudelin. I didn't care what I did. I had George with me. I better do it first or somebody will be in here knocking me on my ass and do it before me. It seems to me people don't feel that way as much. It's a sad thing. It's not good and it isn't necessary. I don't think the whites and the blacks are going to ever get along that well anyway, but at least you'll be able to work and trust the guys they work with. Now it almost like both races are trying to screw each other. The blacks are trying to screw the white. The whites are trying to screw the blacks. That's horrible for a job like this.

Pianka: When I went to Belmont Avenue, not only did I work with black people in the community, but in the fire house. Boisey Cosby was there, Elton Fisher. Belmont Avenue was probably at the time one of the more integrated firehouses. There weren't that many blacks on the job to that point. It didn't start really, yes, until they changed the testing and they made an active effort to bring blacks on the job. My personal opinion, to this day I think they did the right thing. This is a black community, black neighborhood; you have to have colored people, people of the neighborhood on this job. I remember Boisey telling me when he first came on the job in the early '60s, late '50s, they weren't too well received. You know how firemen are. They're just tough. There were times that he came up to the bunk room and the mattress of the bed that was assigned to him was out in the backyard or out on the roof. It was busting balls, but at the root of it you know that it was a black white issue. Over the years guys got over with that because they realized Boisey's a good guy and the other black fellows, the guys realized they were decent firemen. They were the guys who paved the way on this job for the rest of the black guys.

I wasn't really paying that much attention to other ethnic groups. You knew there were a lot of Irish and German on the job because historically and traditionally that's what this job was. But it wasn't rammed down your throat. It wasn't, "Hey, the big lug's a Polack." It was no big deal. The biggest dichotomy was black white for obvious reasons. Now over the years that's diminished quite a bit. In one sense because people work together and they realize neither side are a bunch of ogres. That's how you get over things, by working together. There are other things that bother people, but that's understandable too. You know the testing and the changing in the so-called standards which to me never made much sense anyway. Hey, all you need on this job are a pair of balls, work like a donkey, and be willing to do what they tell you. That's all. It doesn't take much more than that.

T. Grehl: The consent decree started to change the morale. When I first came on, to my knowledge there was no issue of race anything. Nationality, it never came into play. Consent decree, guys started thinking, "Well, I might not have advancement for promotions because of it." The original one, we were going to have two lists. We were going to have a minority list and we were going to have a regular list. That started playing into a lot of people's minds. How did it affect morale? I really don't know. You'd really have to research the overall thing. I just read something the other day that we're still no where near our quota of what we're supposed have, as far as to meet the consent decree. But the morale started changing. Started changing in that respect a little, but again it started changing in different parts of the city. Twelve Engine was an all-black crew on our tour other than the captain and they were the greatest bunch of guys. So, we had no animosity towards them.

Are we lowering the standards? Yes, that bothered people because now you thought you were taking a certain type of job and dropping it down and not getting as intelligent people on. But Boisey was there. He invited me to a New Year's Eve party at his house. There was no animosity. And I would have gone except I had other plans. I would have stopped by. He lived in the middle of Newark. I had no problem with that.

My morale wasn't changed, but you could see where it was going to be changed for the future because of the changing of the structure, not necessarily individuals.

Ryan: Was the consent decree necessary? I don't know. I think the natural progression of the city population would have probably taken care of it. I really do. The city has always been a city of immigrants. Unfortunately, it takes a twenty-five to thirty year progression before another generation goes through the fire department. That's the length of your career. Yes, with whatever population you have in a majority in the city, it becomes assimilated into the fire department. At the turn of the century it was Germans and Irish and remained that way pretty much. But that was the majority of the people.

In the '60s you started to get a large influx of African-Americans into the city, a lot. It takes time for this to be digested. When you're the majority of the people of one ethnicity, you're going to by just natural progression and numbers be represented on the fire department or whatever, but it doesn't happen overnight. Because the guys they're hiring today, they may be of a completely different ethnic group at the end of their career than the people who are in the majority in the city. We see a large Hispanic influx into the city now and we're starting to see that coming on the fire department.

It's hard to figure out, because it's only open to residents to take the exam. If you're going to be a resident, fine. I'll compete against anybody in anything. Always felt that way. I've sat in the same schoolroom with every variety known to man, never had any problem. In the next ten or twenty years we may be a predominantly Hispanic city, but the same guys who are coming on the job now will be of a different ethnic or racial group than what will be the majority of the city. You can't really change it. Sure there are laws and there are changes and there are population shifts, but the one thing that's static is this guy's got to put twenty-five to thirty years on the job, no matter how the city changes.

That's true until the openings start occurring and more people from the new group start applying. Then you'll see a natural progression of the department and up through the ranks, just by sheer numbers. I can't say it often enough, through out the history of the city, it has always been a city of immigrants. Whether they're internal immigrants from other parts of the United States or they're from a different country. I don't see it changing.

Langenbach: The consent decree caused a lot of bitterness because this was another thing that just wasn't understood. A firehouse is a great place for rumors to fester. Good ones and bad ones. And of course it went around the firehouse that this was just like a token. We're just going to give the job, just give the job away. And it was called "the job". Because everybody still had that "This is our job. This is our place. You're not going to give my job away. It's our job. This is what we worked for all these years." It's almost like your getting this passed on from the generations before you. "I've got to protect it like the Holy Grail. You can't just give this away. You've got to earn it. I had to earn it."

So there were a lot of bad feelings about it and a lot of things could have been avoided if they were explained better to people. But they weren't. It seemed like, "We're going to force this down your throats. The courts said we can do this, so we're going to do it." I never understood the bad feelings about it because it didn't make any difference. If a smart white kid and a not so smart minority kid compete, the white kid's still going to win. They didn't selectively say, "Okay, you're going to take one test and I'm going to take another test." Everybody took the same test. It just changed the opportunity.

I don't think I ever saw it, but I heard of times when there was discrimination on this job, when people were discriminated against. I know that Captain Conlin loved Richie Freeman and hated Wayne Rosetti. He didn't like Italians. Before Wayne he had Mike Miele. Mike was a fireman at Twelve just before I got there and then Wayne came there and Red didn't like Italians. He liked Richie Freeman. Richie Freeman did a good job for him. Wayne did a great job for him, but that was the Irish Italian thing. The Irish didn't trust Italians. But I know people were forced to eat elsewhere. I heard all those stories. It didn't make any sense to me, but that's what was done.

Connell: The black and white issue, it's already more divisive in the job right now than it was twenty-five years ago. You actually hate where the fire department is breaking off into segments. You try to work together for the good of the whole department, but everybody's worrying about their own special interest groups. That's a big thing on the morale. I'm not saying all of them are like that. There are lots of exceptions to it. There are a lot of good guys out there and there are a lot of assholes.

Perdon: I don't think the consent decree was necessary, not to the extent that they did it. Things would have had to change. It would have changed. They were in the process. The test was changing. I probably took the easiest physical. Everything was changing at that point in '74 as far as your entrance, but once they got involved in the promotional, I thought they over stepped their boundaries. That's just for common sense reasons.

They say we went through all the books studying. A lot of this stuff you learned in the book is useless. But you know what, if you're going to put yourself in a position where you're going to be a captain of a company, some of that useless information, you should have to know it. You never know when you're going to need it. When you started doing the other test after the government got involved with the testing, they were limiting what you really had to know or what you should know. I thought they over stepped themselves.

As far as the entrance, it was changing. Even now, if you don't put your time in, if you don't get ready for the physical, you won't do well. No matter how they change it, the numbers aren't to where it makes them happy. It's just a matter of application. If you study, you're going to do well. But once again, once they got involved in the promotional, there's nobody going to convince me that was right.

It bothered a lot of people. It bothered me. I was number two and they threw the test out, but being where I was stationed made it easy for me to get over that. I was with good people and I wasn't going to let my problem affect that company, because that company was too good. So, I went to work everyday just like, "Yes, sure I know I just got screwed." But I couldn't and wouldn't let it affect my personal work with that company. Because you're busy it takes your mind off a lot of different things. You're surrounded by good people. You kept that type of stuff in control. But the morale did get affected and rightfully so. I couldn't fault anybody for having a gripe with it and I didn't fault anybody for accepting it. It was a matter of preference, personal preference.

There was friction there. You always heard about it. You would hear individual stories about two guys butting heads. But these were just two people. The Vulcans in arguing it, they were at odds. Every time you met each other, it just didn't pan out like that all the time. Is the friction there? Yes, but it was kept in check for the most part, especially at a fire. It was ignored. The subject wasn't brought up.

On occasion people would talk about it, about the consent decree and the testing. If they would try something off the wall like you can't lay off blacks. You can only lay off the white guys. You would look at them and say, "What is that all about?" But short of that, pretty much it was kept in check from everybody that I know. I've seen individuals on both sides that are just going to be that way. They're going to be confrontational.

I've seen it on the fire scene, on occasion, but I don't know if it was a black and white thing, just a hotheaded individual, who was just known to have quick hands period. It was a black and white fight, but I don't think it had anything to do with black and white issues. But other than that, it's like I tell the guys in my company, I defy anybody to tell me what color the man is standing next to you in a fire building if they don't open their mouth. If they're there in the dark, in the smoke, and they don't say anything, all you know is that you're happy that they're there. If you see anything, all you know is it's a blue uniform and turnout gear and he's happy that he's there, black, white, whatever. That's what I say. I'll hate you maybe outside, but inside you're my best buddy and I'm your best buddy no matter what color you are. I'm just happy that you're there. That's the way I always looked at it. I mean, Richie Freeman, to me was one of the best guys I know.

Bisogna: I didn't come across any ethnic firehouses. Maybe I was just naïve. I've always been a little bit naïve as far as discrimination goes. I couldn't believe people would be like that. My buddy was Irish, and I said, "What's with your father? He never really cared for me. When I come to get you, your father's a grump. What's his problem?" And the kid's answer was, "Well, you're Italian. My father doesn't really care for Italians." I was nineteen or twenty at the time and I was taken back. I didn't think there was that kind of animosity between Irish and Italians and Germans and stuff. I know when my father first came on the job, there were problems. I really didn't experience it, but I think my father did. As far as being an Italian, getting called names going into a firehouse with a German captain and an Irish buddy of his and they picked on my old man. I've heard stories from older guys about that, but I didn't run into it.

But then again, my first captain was Italian. There were Caufields and Giorgios and everybody got along. I have to give that to Twenty Engine. I don't think anybody in that house held anything against me. There might have been a few old timers who said, "Another Italian on the job." But I didn't feel that way at all. In fact I was even surprised to hear about black discrimination. Don't get me wrong, I knew it was there. Boisey Cosby was one of the first blacks in Twelve Engine. His first night they threw his mattress out the window. To say, "Get out of here." I was naïve to a lot of that. Even in Vailsburg above the Parkway there weren't that many racial problems because you really didn't have that many blacks around. It was a little different back then. People kept to where they lived. There wasn't the same demand for rights and step on my tail type of thing back then. Maybe they felt it, but I didn't notice it. I'm not the brightest guy on the block.

But later on the morale went down for several reasons. Affirmative action was, I don't want to say jammed down our throats, but the captain's list they threw out was the first test I could take. I think I was on the job ten years. They needed officers and they gave a test and then there was a lot of controversy about it. A lot of arguing back and forth at the firehouse, which wasn't accomplishing anything, but guys were hurt by the attitude of the fire department, not so much the fire department as the state. You're going to take this right or wrong. We've got to rectify this problem that we have. It's an obvious problem and you are the guys who are going to be made to suffer.

A lot of guys swallowed that pill bitterly. I think at that point guys said, "Well, you know what? I'm going to come in when I feel like it. I'm not going to work as hard." There was definitely a change in the attitude as far as even going to fires. Guys weren't running up the stairs anymore. They were taking guys out of different firehouses and making you work minimum role call, one and two was standard. It was a long time before I said, "Hey, you know what? They're really giving us overtime and they wanted us to be one and three." We were one and two all the time.

Every November we got a pink slip for, how long was that? Five, six, seven years in a row? Before you got laid off, they had to notify you forty days in advance if there might be layoffs. So, everybody got a layoff notice and that definitely took a lot out of the job. It was probably not even that one thing that did it, the captain's list or affirmative action, but a snowballing effect of a number of things that got under guys' skin. It seemed that the Director or Fire Chief weren't on your side anymore. Making you work with minimum manpower and older equipment. The City was failing in its job to support us and it did show up.

The camaraderie suffered, but not in every firehouse. There were still groups that it didn't matter what happened, but the peripheral, the slower firehouses probably suffered more. There you got guys saying, "To hell with it. I'm getting the same pay as the guy going to a million fires. I don't care." You got a lot of that. Guys threw their hands up. And a lot of arguing amongst each other about affirmative action and the throwing the list out and this is bullshit. So much so that I had to walk out of the room a number of times. I said, "Look we're not solving anything by getting our blood pressure going here." So, I would just leave. Whoever wanted to get miserable, go ahead and get miserable. I couldn't live that way. It did affect the morale of the fire department.

I hope the consent decree controversy has hit a plateau and now everyone's accepting it. I know in my case it has. The only thing I thought at the time was, okay it was a multiple choice test. It was geared to a guy who went to high school and was trained for these multiple choice tests. And I will grant you that the language that was used might be difficult to the kids who grew up going through the Newark school system. I went to Catholic schools, but the guys who went to the public schools would have had a harder time and because of the words, just a simple word on a question. If you didn't understand the vocabulary meaning of a word in a question, how can you answer the question? And there were a lot of good points as far as that went. The only thing that I disagreed with was we're going to make the test easier for the people who went to the Newark school system and rightly so, to attain the job, but they want the job handed to them, because they might have been slighted in the past. Not them, but their fathers or whatever. They wanted to be the captains in a minute and they wanted to be chiefs like they were owed everything. I took my first captain's test after ten years on the job. I did well and then they threw it out on me. I was pissed. But I would rather have them throw it out than to insert guys unfairly in there.

There were arguments. The guys who were up front on that list; who were in the top twenty, they didn't mind if there was going to be random insertions of minorities. That's the only phrase you can use because that's what they were going to do. They didn't mind because that's where they were. They were fifteen so if they put three guys in before them they were only number eighteen. It was the guys in the forties and fifties who thought it was unfair because now you're putting ten guys before me. I don't get promoted. So, fifteen doesn't care because he's only getting promoted a couple of months later, but number fifty does because he's not getting promoted at all. So, I was glad to see it thrown out at that point because of all the discussions going back and forth. You had guys, good friends, who were yelling at each other about it, all depending on where they sat on the list. It's funny how it worked out, every fourth or fifth guy was a minority, but at least it was a redo and everybody had a new shot at the shuffle.

There are still problems on this job though as far as racial mixes and stuff. I think it's all over. I don't know if it's individuals. I mean there are definitely individuals out there in both races or let's say in all races who don't like somebody else. But there are white guys who don't like the way another white guy looks. It doesn't matter what color you are; sometimes the personalities just don't mix.

Ricca: On the new test, I had the fourth highest written in the state because twelve other towns had taken the promotional test. Eli Savarese said, "Ronnie, forget about it. You got to fall on your head not to make captain." I knew my rank after the written portion of the test because information supposedly leaked out. The way I understand it, they changed the marking system. They changed it from groups to individual marking and then they weighed everything on the second half, the interview. The interview I didn't do badly on, but I didn't do that well on it, so I came out thirty-six. This goes on eight years before I get promoted in 1989.

Every day a different story and everybody being in limbo, and the friction between the guys who were on the list, the minorities who would have gotten promoted and between the guys that would have been promoted had they kicked in a campaign contribution. Just went back and forth, back and forth. It was a mess. Calvin Jackson never took the second test. He was so disgusted. He was a genuinely good fireman and a studier. He deserved it. There are a couple of black guys on that list who were studiers who got hurt, that didn't get promoted because of the way things happened.

After I was promoted I had a black crew. I didn't find differences in how other companies treated us in the Fourth Battalion because they all had a reputation. Even to this day I have a mixed crew and I never think of Ray being Puerto Rican and Don being black. I think of them as firemen and they treat me as the captain. I think that's why it works out. But Boisey, I heard stories of him when he was at Five Truck when he first came on. As he walked out into the court yard, they'd throw his mattress out the window. But not once did Boisey ever have a bad word to say to me.

We had a fire in the back of Ten Truck. Fire blowing up the steps, Boisey popped his gloves on, put his mask on, and walked down the steps. I looked at one of the guys and I said, "Are you going to go down now?" It was hot and we went down. We were burning up. Boisey was just going in there. After that this guy said, "I take back everything I ever said." Because he realized Boisey's a fireman. That's the whole thing. That's the only thing I want from this job. Somebody to say, "Yeah, he was a good fireman." when you leave. You don't want somebody saying, "Yeah, he was a piece of shit, a shit head or whatever." That's how I treated those guys and that's how they treated me. Never, not once, not once was any racial undertone ever even thought of.

Gesualdo: I just don't think I was really high enough for the consent decree to have affected my career. I was in the eighties, so I probably wouldn't have gotten made, but I always remember feeling very upset about certain individuals having put the time in and then have the list thrown out. I remember George Perdon, Kevin Burkhardt, Pat Durkin and Vinney Kuhn, all these individuals. I know they probably were studying for years because I was only on the job for two years when it came up. And thinking that what motivates these people, because they were still great firefighters, these guys didn't let that bother them. So, I think by seeing them reacting the way they did, it just made me feel like "Hey this is fate. This is life." And you go on. I definitely know I admired these individuals tremendously for carrying on the way they did. A lot of people would have said, "To hell with it." Went to quieter companies, quieter parts of the city, thrown their hands up and said forget about it. So that's what I remember more, not from a personal point of view. It didn't affect me all that much. I was working part time, a steady part time job, so it wasn't a money issue. I always knew I wanted to be a captain, but I figured I've got time. It was the other individuals I felt for more than myself.

I remember that being probably one of the most confrontational periods in my career, mostly between different races, ethnic groups there was a lot of, I shouldn't say hostility, but malice maybe, friction. A lot of the minorities were glad the test got thrown out, that kind of like upset some of the other individuals who did put the time in and caused quite a few problems and riffs. It seemed like there were a lot of transfers going on at the time and people wanting to get out of certain situations because of certain individuals in the firehouse.

That was probably one of the most difficult periods, late '70s, early '80s when that test got thrown out and the consent decree come in because I think the majority of people on the job at that point didn't feel there was that much in the way of discrimination. It might have been prior, but is there discrimination now because blacks run the city? You'd probably get a lot of white guys who say there is. The same as you'd get a lot of black guys back then who said there was discrimination because whites ran the city or were in charge of the city. So, I think for the most part that was a non-issue. I think it was just a lot of individuals who didn't prepare properly or didn't want to take the time to prepare. Figured they could just get it through creating a disturbance. That's the way I feel about it. I don't think it was with the consent decree. But things haven't been the same since the consent decree.

I think the racial mix of the department would be there without the consent decree. There might not be as many blacks in command positions. I don't think the consent decree is responsible for getting more minorities. It didn't have an effect on the enrollment as far as firefighters in the initial capacity on the fire department. It was going to happen. The evolution was going to happen eventually. You have more in command positions because of the consent decree. Whether it's right or wrong, they're there. But whether they really deserved the positions or not is still a matter of question. It always will be, unfortunately. Because you know there are some who have prepared and who had studied and you could see it. You could see it in any group. There are captains of all different backgrounds and races. You could see that some of them weren't prepared and they're there because of the restructuring of the exam.

I was always confused about the consent decree, even having been involved with the hiring and training and all that for quite a while, I still really don't understand it. The interpretation of it fluctuates. One court appearance you'll hear one interpretation. I was under the impression it was a goal with sixty percent application rate. That's the way I read it. Now, other people will tell you, "Oh, it's sixty percent hiring." I didn't read it that way, but I think without the consent decree, you'd be in the same position you're in now. Because the racial numbers of the city are increasing and a lot of people will also forget to include Hispanics sometimes in that equation. With the Hispanics and black that are coming on, we're probably very close to the consent decree requirements, whether it's hiring or application.

Chapter Four: Job Changes

Fredette: You eliminated those portable oil stoves, but started getting electrical fires, fires caused by televisions and radios, and carelessness as the homes kept on deteriorating. Naturally as a home gets older there's more chance of a fire starting with the wires. Then there was aluminum siding, which slowed down a lot of fires. We used to have asphalt siding. When you go in there the whole side was going like hell. All you really needed was a sweep over it with a two and a half inch. You could go from the ground up and knock that right down. You also had to cover the house next door. The buildings in a lot of these fires were close to one another. You couldn't just get in and put that fire out; you had to stop it from getting next door. One line in the alleyway could take care of both houses. Maybe the other one had asphalt siding. Maybe the fire was not as bad as it looked. It was just the siding going.

They started cutting down the size of the companies. We had over eight hundred firemen at one time, not including officers. You would have one officer and four men on a company. I remember Twenty Engine had two pieces and rode one and seven.

Vetrini: The company fire brigades down along Doremus Avenue were tremendous. They were excellent. As the years went on and you pulled into these companies where they had a situation, you had personnel there who were able to tell you what was what and had already taken some action. Prior to that; everybody would be standing outside waiting for you. Maybe you would have some people, but it was not like a supervised situation. It was maybe a fellow who had more responsibility and took it upon himself to do this or do that.

There were fires in the paint companies, Benjamin Moore and Sherwin-Williams. From my memory, those two companies always seemed to have some sort of supervision, if you want to call it a fire brigade. House keeping in those two companies was excellent. I don't recall if we had a real major fire. You had varnish pots. One of their pots would go. They always had their equipment around there already. It wasn't that they could contain it. A lot of times they would take their standpipes. They would have hose out there already.

The city's population changed in number and in the people who were in the city. A lot of the old families moved out and other people moved in. There was a lot of carelessness. There is no question about it. That's what created a lot of the fires that we had; carelessness. Years before people were more careful. We didn't have the situations that were created later on.

Kinnear: Significant changes, first we had shorter hours which gave the men more freedom. I think if you ever had those long hours today, even a fifty-six hour week, you'd have almost chaos in the department because guys would be going crazy. That was the big thing, shorter hours.

Of course, in the number of personnel, the low roll calls, that's been a significant difference. It's a significant factor. I think it's dangerous both to the public and the firemen. You're one or two men short riding on an apparatus. You can't do half the work that a one and four can do. You do maybe one third or one quarter of the work that a full crew can do. It doesn't work proportionately. If you take a man away it doesn't decrease the company strength by twenty-five percent. It decreases it by maybe fifty percent because it's teamwork. You've got to work together. You lose one man and your crew is broken up. The lack of personnel has definitely effected the department greatly.

Vesey: You're dealing with some people in different sections of Newark. The Latinos are coming on now and the Portuguese. That's all changed. You see the city you were born and raised in all of the sudden changing. You've seen it right in front of you. So your attitude has to change. Not saying as far as firefighting. You put the fire out and make an effort to get anybody in there, but the whole country changed.

Masters: I think the major change was when we got fewer hours, so we could spend more time at home. I think that was important. Because being away from the family twenty-four hours and more was hard. When they cut the hours down, that was good.

F. Grehl: The change in hours worked and the remuneration you received as far as pay, holidays, and all the other things. The changes as far as doing the job, it'll always be the same. You still have to have the manpower to do the job. You still have to have the equipment. The city probably kept up pretty well with equipment. I would say, basically, they were five years ahead of the rest of the country. From the time Sommers took over, they were always really on top of it. He was a very aggressive man and the rest of the chiefs after him have been aggressive. So, we've always been ahead as far as the equipment goes. They've been willing to go out and buy new things, to try new things, and try new practices. The old timers like Ruscheck would say, "No, no, you don't use that. No, no." He would never even try it. But we've always had people who were willing to try.

Less companies today; thirty engine companies, there were a lot of engine companies. We're down to about nineteen. With the rotational closings now you have it down around sixteen actually working on a given day. It's one good tactical, political way of reducing four companies. You see what happened. The fellows grunted and groaned and made a lot of noise, but what's happening? The fires are still going out. Vince Greeley always used to say, "Hey, all the fires go out. You see any fires burning that started years ago. They're all out. We do it. We put them out. Sometimes it takes a little longer, but we put them out."

The first company I was assigned to had one officer and seven men. That was a way they hid people who were injured. We had one fellow with Parkinson's disease. I guess times were a little different. They could take care of people long term rather than put them out to pasture. I would say they had a tough time because you were working that many hours in the firehouse. We never had one and seven, at best one and five. When we went to the fifty-six hour workweek, a lot of companies dropped to one and four, one and five. The busier companies they tried to give one and five. Two piece companies they tried to give one and five. There were ten two-piece companies in the city at one time. Then when we went to the forty-two hour workweek, everybody had one and four.

Somewhere along the line they decided to go to manpower units. They had two of them. They went to one and eight. Twenty Engine and One Engine were both two-piece companies, so they gave them one and eight. They were supposed to be manpower companies that could be specially called. They ran their regular assignments, too. But you can't sit with eight people there and two people in Six Engine. So, the next thing you know a detail was made, eventually that died, too. There are economics involved. You have to expect it to die. They need people.

McCormack: Roll calls when I first came on generally were one and four; that was the standard. There was always a couple of one and threes around for one reason or another, but the majority of your companies were one and four. Once in a blue moon after something major happened, maybe there was a fire where a bunch of guys got injured, someone might be riding one and two, but it was extremely rare.

Back then it was against the rules to moonlight. There was a section in the rulebook that said, "All firemen shall devote their entire time and effort to the prospects of the Newark Fire Department." or something like that. That was in the rulebook when I came on. So they subsisted on their pay. That changed sometime in the '60's. The administration at that time changed the rulebook. They dropped out any prohibitions about working part time. So, that opened up all kinds of possibilities. You could do a lot of things they were hesitant to do before.

Then there was the advent of the two-income family. When I first came on the job no woman worked. Women did not work. I mean a married woman stayed home. She was a housewife and a mother. A woman who worked in those days was frowned upon by society. Obviously, there was something wrong with her husband if he couldn't take care of her. It was his responsibility to take care of her. If she had to go out and get a job there was something wrong with him. He wasn't doing the right thing as a man, as a husband, to take care of his wife. The women would work up until the time they got married and maybe they'd work until the time the first child came along, but once they had their first child that was the end of their working career. In that era women did not work. There were a few women in the telephone company and few places like that, a few schoolteachers. Women were traditionally schoolteachers in those days. World War II changed all that with the "Rosie the Riveter" syndrome. We found out that women could do practically anything men could do, but before that it wasn't believed that way.

Those were some of the things that changed the economic condition of the firemen, the allowance to let them do other things and the two-income family. Today women get paid what men get paid. Today most homes have two full incomes coming in, not only on the fire department, outside the fire department, too. Women work. They put their children out to day care centers or whatever. Somebody else takes care of their kids and they go to work. They double the income. Sometimes the women make more than their husbands, so they're better off. I hear firemen talking today saying, "Oh, yeah, I took a cruise. I went to Bermuda. I went to Vegas. I went to Germany. I toured Europe. I went to Taiwan." If you got down to the Jersey shore, to Keyport, to Keansburg for a week in the summer time you were rich in those days. I mean "Oh, my God. This guy's wealthy. He took his family down and rented a bungalow in Keansburg for a week." Forget about cruises, the movie stars went on cruises.

There have been improvements in the pension act. They reduced the retirement age. Guys are making more money today. They're able to get Social Security today if they qualify for it on the outside. They also have the annuity plans and things within the fire department now that sweeten up the pie. A lot of the wives are working and can collect Social Security. So, things are a lot better today than they were then, yes. Economically, they're a heck of a lot better.

Masterson: The uniform, we wore khaki pants and chambray shirts. Then they came out with the blue uniform. I never ever saw that order. I came back from vacation. All of the sudden I see these guys wearing these blue shirts, blue pants. What the hell was going on? That was a change.

Deutch: The change I didn't care for was the manpower change, where you did more work. You didn't have the men riding with you. There were times when you were riding one and two and get a fire. That was unheard of. Plus they closed firehouses. There were twelve truck companies and over thirty engine companies. At times we were riding one and five and then we'd have the volunteers riding with us. There wasn't a spot on that apparatus. You had to fight for a spot.

The latest manpower change I would never go for. That is taking the driver away from the chief. I can't understand how a city can run like that because I've seen drivers save lives at fires. One of the best chief's drivers I ever saw was my captain, Captain McCoy, before he was promoted. He did more truck work and engine work while he was driving the chief.

The splitting of the union was another change. We were all under one union years ago. Then the officers got their own union. We had our own. They always went for raises on their own. In the old days it was always the same raise. That's why the captains never climbed more than six hundred ahead of us. They didn't get the percentage raises. Then the city thought, "Well, let's break them down. We can talk to the firemen and not worry about the officers being against us." All the police and fire unions were all broken up, officers and firemen, officers and patrolmen. That was a big change. That occurred in the '60s somewhere. Because right after that, the captains got their raise and they went like twenty two hundred ahead of us which I always thought they earned. Six hundred was not enough for that job because they had to write all the reports and have all the headaches.

Another thing is when I came on you worked for one Director of Public Safety. Director Keenan was our director, Police and Fire. Then they changed that pretty soon, too. In the old days you just called it working for public safety. That was a big thing when they changed that. Then I guess the Director was a business administrator. In our old days it was all businessmen who were your director. After the Keenan regime went out, that seemed to change.

Wall: There was an interim period there where Caufield had gone against the mayor and Caufield was out. Redden was Chief slash Director. During that period we changed a lot of protocols. In fact, that's when we changed the uniforms. We developed the bell hats and changed the work uniform. Before, we used to wear khaki pants. Stanley Kossup and I ran the committee. We made the contacts with the clothing manufacturer, tested different materials, and we ended up with this uniform. So when Caufield came back, he was really pissed off. Things had changed on the department when he was gone and we weren't loyal to him and all this other business.

Freeman: I think OSHA coming out with their standards has made it better. Before, we had to buy our own coats. We had to buy our own gloves. We had to buy our own helmets. There were no standards. You could use anything you wanted. Now everything is to OSHA standards, which is good. Plus the city issues you equipment now and you have to give it back. So that's a big change right there.

Firefighting techniques are better. Training is better. You have more training now than we ever had. Training has been major. I think there should be more training. I'm all for training because that's the only way you're going to know, especially now with fires being down. You don't get the training, the fire ground training that we got many years ago. So, the training is definitely a major change.

Before, you didn't have that kind of training. You didn't have any training at all really because we didn't have a training ground, Eighteenth

Avenue that was it. And the only other way would be the captains in the companies. They did train us, the captains in the companies, but a formal training area, no. So I think this was a plus. I think we should do much, much more training. The guys don't like it, but it can save their lives and also other's lives.

Those are the basic changes, especially training. In the later years you've had drug problems. It's up to the captain to address that. However, if it keeps up he should take care of it. A lot of guys don't. They just take care of their own. I don't think that should be, but I'm not their captain. If it was me it wouldn't be because I think it's a detriment to my guys who are straight and this guy is not. It could cause one of my guys, the straight guy, to lose his life maybe. You're not getting any help from him.

McGee: An important change is the effect of the job on your family life; most guys had to work part time because the pay was low at that time. Actually the pay didn't really get good until about ten years before I retired, most of the time it was well below what the average person was making. That being the case, most worked. If you had any children in private school, like I did, you had to work. I worked quite a bit. I worked at all kinds of jobs, whatever came around.

McGrory: The major change I've seen is the fire department being weaned down so much. That's probably a big major change. It went from ten, eleven hundred people down to seven something. That's a lot of loss of firehouses, loss of personnel. Do they have the coverage? I hate to see one and two because I know what job you have to do and I know it can't be done. There were changes in firefighting tactics and changes in buildings, changes in building materials and in the laws. You can go on and on and on and on. One is just as important as the other. But to affect the average guy on the fire department, I'd say the unions' coming in was the greatest change. Then there were the different administrations in the city, which affects you ever minute of your working day or night. A big, big thing with firefighters was changes in the attitudes of people.

We had a lot of changes. When I came on the job when we came back from runs in rainy weather, we had to wash under the rigs no matter what time of the night. If there was a multiple alarm of fire in, you had to hit the floor.

Denvir: Significant changes, cutting down on the runs. The signal nine with the two engines and one truck cut down on the runs, although there are a lot of runs. We still get a lot of runs, but it did cut back with all the false alarms.

Freda: The biggest difference in the job is everyone couldn't wait to go to work years ago. It was fun. There were a lot of fires. Much more work than they have today. There was a lot of camaraderie. There was a lot of fun in the firehouse. You couldn't wait to get out the door of your house some nights and go to work. It was someplace in the world to go and enjoy yourself. I don't think that anyone on the job today will say that they really can't wait to come to work. I think the job has changed that much for various reasons. Not too many people worked part time in those days, moonlighting. Now everybody does it. I think that's changed. This has become their second job.

Before the '50s, no one in the fire department used any kind of mask except the Rescue Squad. I know this from people I talked with. I'm fortunate. When I came on the job there were still some old timers who went back twenty and thirty years prior to1959 who told me a lot of stories about how the fire department was. The job of the Rescue Squad then was that the engine companies would stretch in and attack the fire. When the Rescue Squad showed up, they would take the line from you and continue extinguishing the fire and you would leave the building.

Charpentier: Discipline has become very lax. The day I came on the job and prior to the day I came on the job, I knew there were rules and regulations. I went out of my way to make sure I abided by them. Fortunately, I was never brought up on charges. I never caused anything to be done, a few automobile accidents which we've had with the apparatus. The two that we had were found not to be our fault. But the disciplinary actions today from what it was ten or fifteen years ago are very lax in almost all incidents.

Smith: Significant changes? When they started reducing the manpower; they took away the two-piece companies; which was a big mistake, then the gradual reduction in manpower. A captain and five men can work at a hundred percent of efficiency. Now you have a captain and three men, did each one of those remaining men become roughly forty percent stronger? No, no. Something has to give.

Another thing that stands out in difference between when I came on and now is they won't allow you to improvise. You can't improvise on the fire ground. Years ago, everybody knew their job, really knew their job. Whatever innovative measure they had to take at a fire, they took. Let me give you an example. I was driving the engine one time and I had a good hydrant. The fire was on a dead end and they weren't getting any pressure. So what I did was take two lines, two and a half inch, opened up the two inch and a half outlets on a hydrant up the street from the fire and opened the stem of that hydrant. I had the four and a half hooked up to my hydrant and I stretched back to another hydrant with an additional two and a half. Then I pumped into that hydrant, so that the companies hooked up to the bad hydrants on the end would have water.

Miller: When I came on the job there was an eight o'clock roll call. You had to be in uniform and you had to line up. After that you started your housework. There was no time to read the papers, to come in and bull shit. Chiefs would come around and inspect you at a certain time and they were there every day. The captain would inspect to make sure you were okay. Today, it's a little more lax. I don't know if it's good or it's not. It was more autocratic then. Today it's a more democratic or liaise faire attitude. I think a lot of the captains have that attitude. They just don't care. They're going to get away with doing the least they can.

I don't believe in doing things autocratically. I think it should be a combination of humanistic, democratic, and autocratic, depending on the individual. But since we're a semi-military organization, we should tighten up a little bit. The officers definitely should start housework by eight-thirty. Everybody should be in uniform, completely dressed, shaved, and housework should start. It should be done in a professional manner. It should take an hour, that's all. If everybody chips in, you have the rest of the day for reading, drills, or whatever you want to do. Nobody asks that much of you on the job. Even as bad as housework was when I came on the job we did everything in two hours. No one bothered you after that. You could do it and the house was clean. It was a morale booster because you took pride. You had a clean house. Actually people competed. Whose house was the cleanest? God, you'd go to a house on detail. You'd come back and you'd talk. "Boy that was a dirty house. Don't they clean?" In that respect it's a change and I think it should go back to more of a semi-military organization. That has to start with the captains. They have to enforce it more.

With modern firefighting techniques, you can get water on the fire quicker. The apparatus is so much better today; personnel are better trained than they ever were on the fire department. But will they remember what they were trained to do? You can't blame the staff if they don't remember. They do the best they can. It's a highly qualified staff of training personnel. They give a good training program.

The personnel and the equipment will lead to a better fire department and maybe less equipment. You can do with fewer engine and truck companies. If I have a piece of equipment that's manned with one and four, it's twice as effective as one and three. They can put more water out just with that extra man. That's in *Fire Attack* and all the books and it's a proven fact, but you have to have the manpower there. The way we're riding today with one and two, one and threes where we were one and fours, it's sad.

The exams have changed in recent years. The quality of the exams has gone down. Prior to that, studying for an exam took a couple of years, three or four hours a day. Every book you could get your hands on, every course you could take including going to other cities to get previous exams because there were always repeat questions. Maybe five percent of every exam they had up to1980 had some repeat questions in the written part. But it's all a form of studying even if you get the repeat questions. If you don't have them, you didn't put the time into it. They did eliminate the physical for the captain's exam, which I didn't think ever was required anyway.

I don't know how many questions they have now on the exam. It used to be a hundred questions, a couple of hours. And it was a well-rounded exam with hydraulics, public relations, supervision, management, a little bit of chemistry, first aid, English, spelling. It was a good exam. Today I don't know what it is.

Dunn: We fight our fires today eighty percent the same as we've fought them all along. I haven't seen what I consider real innovative ideas in firefighting. I base that on the fact that what changed in firefighting are probably the structures, the codes, and private fire protection. If enough of that goes on, you'll see less need for the aggressive, structural type of firefighting that we do. I can go to the numerous things that have changed in the city of Newark. We based our firefighting attack on getting busier every year. Our fire department was programmed that in our conflagration area in the Central Ward, we'd ride companies like Engine Twenty with a one and eight. Lasted a couple of years when they did away with companies.

Even though they were talking about innovative ideas, we were doing the same thing. If we closed down a company today, we'd build up the other manpower and it lasts six months and disappears. The same type of thing was going on at that time.

The tactic in our command structure I thought probably was more effective was based on the companies being together as a unit longer. You just worked together better. So, your tactic was different because you knew what you were dealing with as far as your manpower. Today we're in an area where I ride the second and third busiest company in Newark as a one and one roll call. Every night the captain is riding with his make up crew, so the tactics of that company just don't fit into the mainstream of the fire department ten years ago because you have a different crew there. Different men react differently to every fire situation. There was a drill in the academy today with a live fire burn. They brought Eleven Engine down. You wound up with a man from Fourteen Engine, a guy from Seven Engine and a driver, so the guy that did the drill today was the captain. He didn't have enough information on two overtime firemen to say "Listen, I'll do one crew; you do the next crew." The same thing would happen at a fire here. The captain would become the key component of the company because he's the only guy he trusts right now. Ten years ago we didn't have that kind of problem. We didn't have this make up, change of shift going on; where we don't know day to day who's in our fire companies. I'll bet you today we have five or six units running with no more than one original man in it. So, that is certainly something you would have to put into an equation to say "Is our firefighting good?"

Harris: I think the major changes are the deterioration of the equipment that we have, the reduction in the manpower we have, and the fact that the administration appears to not care about the firefighting force or the manpower that we have. In the Arson Squad, we are driving two vehicles around that have over a hundred and twenty-five thousand miles on them. This is ridiculous. We can't get a car. We got the van, but that was from somebody else and they gave it to us.

You watch engine companies break down. We don't have the spares to give them to get them back to quarters. Before, if you had a problem, a mechanic came out, got you started, and got you back to quarters at least to work on. We don't have this anymore. This to me is not the way to run a department. It's not conducive to your life or any fireman's life out there if you have an apparatus that cannot be readily repaired. Radio; years ago, if you had a problem with your radio, they fixed your radio in the street. These are the changes I see that are bad for the department because we're not doing anything that's going to help the men. To me the most important thing that we have is the men. Secondly is the equipment that these men have to use.

Cahill: People who are in charge of buying new equipment should care more about getting the right thing. They should do more research into the masks, the type of masks, things like that. They probably never get everything they like, but I think in that sense there's probably a little more concern about getting good stuff. Not that we always get it, but they should keep trying. Maybe they did in the past. I don't know. Then again morale, there's been a drastic change in that. Sorry to say. And for a whole variety of reasons

Roll calls should be the number one change. We're so much smaller which actually had to change the tactics. It seems we went from an operation with procedures to a "try and get by" operation. That's the best summary I can give you for the overall change.

Highsmith: The major changes? Okay, manpower, clothing, attitudes toward the job, and the slackness from the top on down. Those are the main changes I've seen. But I've also seen fire prevention with seven inspectors do work, I mean work. Work their butts off. I've seen guys in the Arson Squad work hard. When I went to the Arson Squad, there were twenty-three detectives. When I left, there were nine detectives, four captains, one Battalion Chief, and one Deputy Chief. So, those guys are doing work. Everybody is doing much more, even guys out in the field. They're doing much more with much less. That's another big change. And the changes that I've seen that are negative can easily be changed. It has nothing to do with the citizens having their fires put out or with the response of the fire department. It's mostly attitudes.

Butler: Reduction in manpower I think is the biggest on the department. The size of the department, the manpower to drop so drastically; we've lost three hundred firemen. Granted, you've had some companies closed. You lost a lot of companies since I've been on too.

The lack of aggressive attitude by your chief officers and just having the whole thing filter right down. The Deputy doesn't care so if the Deputy doesn't care then the Battalion Chief's not going to worry about it. The Battalion Chief doesn't care; the captain isn't going to care. The captain doesn't give a hoot then the firemen are not really worried about a whole lot of important stuff anymore.

It's just that it's too bad that the general attitude didn't change at the top and work its way down to really build up the morale again. I think it's something that's going to have to be addressed. I don't know when, but the morale is going to have to start being pushed to a point of bringing it up again with the specified lay out for training.

Cody: As far as the firehouses and the way we work, I don't think we've changed. You could come in here thirty-five years later and go right to work because nothing's changed. How you put out a fire, it's the same way. Our equipment is a little bit better, but the tactics are the same. Tactics haven't changed. Not since I've been on anyway. I think if it's not broken, you don't fix it. It seems to be working, so that's the way we do it.

The morale is down. The morale changed on the fire department when they threw out that first captain's list. That was the turning point of the whole fire department as far as morale goes. It was the turning point in the fire department as far as more knowledgeable officers and more knowledgeable firefighters because everyone studied. Even if you didn't get promoted, you still had this knowledge.

Now, you don't see anyone studying. You don't see it. Very, very few guys are studying. They go to a class. They go to the Bernstein class. He tells them, "This is what they're going to ask you." And you go and write it down. Then you go and meet a board, teach a guy how to make a square knot, and you're a captain. It's the same with all the tests now. So, that has to have an effect on morale. There's no competition. It's almost like a lottery system. You could be the smartest guy in the company and come out last. That can't help morale.

Wargo: Major change for one thing, is manpower. I remember when I was down in Eight Truck, if the captain came in and he only had one and two he would go out on a signal five for manpower. Now it's becoming an almost common occurrence. Of course the racial mixture is a lot different. When I came on the job you could probably count the black firefighters on both your hands. Now in every company, every battalion you have black firefighters which reflects the changes.

McGovern: In '74 we got a lot of good, new guys. That's when they opened the test up to state wide. We got a lot of good quality men and it was a big change. They hired a lot of men that year and you had a lot of young blood in the job who wanted to work. A lot of them were vollies in Hoboken and Passaic. You had a lot more ambitious guys who wanted to work. They wanted to learn.

Back when I came on it was get the job done at any cost. Today it's get the job done, but you have to do it safely. Sometimes it's hard to get the job done and do it safely. Today there's such an emphasis on safety. Safety is good, but thinking to get the job done safely is another story. I was thinking of all the times you crawled under power lines to get to a roof or going above a fire, that kind of stuff that we just try not to do anymore

Manpower is another major change. You need more companies to perform the same tasks. In the past, a one and four engine company could always get two lines to work for you. Now you know you're only going to get one line out of a company. They're usually one and two to one and three at the most. Many times in the past, the first due engine company would have a fire out on two floors by the time you got up there. That doesn't happen anymore. That's one of the biggest changes.

Equipment, firefighting gear, and the safety issues are mainly the changes that I've seen. OSHA, that kind of thing, things have to be done a certain way now because it's the law. God help the guy who screws it up. But that's basically the changes. The fires are going to go out no matter what. There are no fires burning right now. It's always been that way. It always will be. They just get bigger and smaller. You don't have the competition you used to have between companies. Now we tend to kind of help each other a little more. This job changes very slowly, very slowly. More slowly than other jobs I think, than the cops or whatever for some reason. Firemen just resent change. They get resistant, in my experience anyway. "It worked for me yesterday; it's going to work for me today." "You got to eat smoke kid." It's the same thing. That's the way they are. It's just part of the job.

Prachar: Some of the changes were to the good; some of them to the bad. The improvements in the department, you've had your good stuff, you've had your bad stuff. Doing away with all the companies, since I'm on this job, which I just started my twenty-fourth year, there have been almost twenty companies put out of service. That's a lot.

Camaraderie could be a big thing to improve. We used to have a lot of camaraderie, now it's not there, but it's starting to come back up hill. You're starting to get people who say, "Look, maybe we could do this here." It will eventually improve, but it's going to take a while.

Finucan: Significant changes on the job? It's a very, very sorry business, the selection process for the city of Newark. But what I see happening is I see an improvement. Everything is like a pendulum. We have seen the worst. They have done the lowest things on the last exams and the last selection process. But each time you get screwed you get a little wiser. So I think that they almost have to be more careful the way they do things in the future. Each test is going to be scrutinized a little more. So I think that maybe starting now, in the last year or two you might start to see some improvements again maybe on the next civil service exam.

The civil service system getting screwed up is one of the major changes since I've been on the job. The discipline falling apart; the old ways being left by the wayside; and the new attitude came in. That's the big difference that I've seen, the general deterioration on the fire department. Tactics are basically the same. We still fight fires from the interior when we can.

McDonnell: They wrecked the captain's exam. They did away with studying. That had a major, major impact. People don't realize it. It didn't affect just the guys who studied. When I was a fireman and I was studying, we constantly talked about fires. It helped everybody because you sat around the table. Even though you weren't studying there were guys there throwing questions at each other and asking, "What's this? What's the angle for a ladder?"

There was an interest in firefighting. There was always that interest in the firefighting that's not there today. They took that away. We lost the knowledge and the competence because of it. People go up the ranks now without knowing a damn thing. Those are the two changes that I see. In my general impression of the department, it went downhill from when I came on. And those are the two reasons.

From my career's start to my finish, one of the biggest changes has been the lack of competence because you're not getting the same type of people. I really believe that. It might not be true, but from my observations that is how I feel. That people don't have it. And there's no knowledge. There's no studying. And they're never going to get it in the present situation.

They think everything is training. How many times can you get them down to the Academy? That's one of the things that the jerks in the Justice Department did. Everything is training. They should be trained to do that. That's a two way street. You can lead a horse to water, but you can't make him drink. That's one of the changes. Then another change in the way of a decline is in the loss of manpower and the loss of companies.

The leadership, wow, what a difference, that's probably the major change on the department from when I came on. The leadership is really lacking in the top, the very top, in the officers, the chief officers. Not the same as it was. You have a few like Jimmy Smith, good as anybody ever was. But thirty years ago there were a bunch of Jimmy Smiths.

The job itself really hasn't changed that much. I mean the actual job. It's the job and the department. The job itself is pretty much the same. It's going to a fire, the same now as it was. You wear different equipment. You do pretty much the same things. Other than that interest in doing the job and the discipline has eroded, it's still a great job. It was a great job then.

That's the thing that always bothered me. Doing what we were supposed to do, it was still a great job. This is like the easiest job in the world. What do you have to work, two hours a day? You have to clean the house, check the rig, and go out and throw a ladder up or stretch a hose and practice. It's a physical skill. There's a mental part to it and there's a physical part. You never lose the mental part. I can know how to raise a ladder. I'll be ninety years old, put an aerial in front of me and I'll raise it, but I won't be able to do anything efficiently. It's a physical thing. It's like sports. If the guys would only take the attitude, you have to practice. What's the big deal? You're sitting in the God damn house. Hoot used to tell us that all the time. No matter what they make you do, you're going to be here ninety percent of the time. So what's the big deal? Other than that the job, is pretty much the same.

Pianka: When I first came on, I remember Five Truck was one and five. Engine Six was one and five. Engine Twenty was one and five. There were still some two-piece companies. They were all one and five. We had a thousand men, over a thousand men. We have half the men now. In my opinion, the best thing you can do at a fire is to throw bodies at it. When Five Truck, Twelve Engine, and at the time we had a Salvage unit, when we went to a first due fire that was within a couple of blocks, you had ten, twelve fifteen guys there, right on the scene, together.

Picture us now. Seven Engine going to a fire and right now we're one and three. You're going to operate with three guys as opposed to fifteen, right off the bat, when it's most important. That's the big difference. I always thought the job was great. I'm essentially doing the same thing. Taking the hose up there and bringing hooks. What's the difference? Fewer bodies.

Right now the workload is a little lower, but it's different. The quality has changed. So, it's not apples to apples. There are two different ways of looking at this fire department. It's changed traumatically in certain ways. This job has always been dangerous, I'm not belittling that. It was dangerous back then. Within a year of when I came on the job, three guys were killed down on Orchard Street, Russell Schoemer, Dominic LaTorre, and Anthony Lardiere. And now we just lost a guy two weeks ago. Manpower is the big difference.

Rotonda: The change in the fire department mechanics as far as maintenance of the equipment has deteriorated terribly. They don't have the mechanics they used to have doing the job they use to do. When the equipment goes to the shop they have to go to another firehouse and borrow the rig of a rotationally closed company. They run around like dogs. It shouldn't be. You have a big city department. They talk about this renaissance and stuff like that. You're making things appear good and they're not as good as they appear. They don't have the maintenance they did. You get a little bit done. It's like scotch taping something and eventually it's all going to fall apart at a disastrous time. That's what they're going to end up with, a disaster. But hey, that's what they want. But that's the biggest change I've seen.

T. Grehl: The work schedule change is major. The short period of time I was in the field with the new schedule, the firemen and officers had split schedules. So, the officers stayed twenty-four and the firemen didn't. The captain stayed twenty-four hours, then he went home and the firemen worked the regular tens and fourteens. So you would work with different guys during the day and at night another shift would come in. That was not advantageous in the fire department. It was much better all being on the same shift in my opinion. Especially when you work with your own crew, a good officer has a fine tuned crew that works together. It's hard enough working with four different personalities, no less twelve or fourteen different personalities in the course of a week.

For the short period of time I was there, the biggest difference was it's a long day. And you have to do something. You just can't sit on the couch and watch cartoons all day long because you're out of your mind. So, probably good things could come about with the twenty-four because you would look forward to maybe doing a little drilling, a little something in the morning, going out and getting lunch. Then you had your study time in the afternoon, but again maybe three thirty, four o'clock, four thirty, five whatever, start preparing dinner. Maybe get together as a unit and start preparing dinner because otherwise it is a long day. It's a long day to be in one location, especially if you're not going out. I can't see it in the slower companies, coming in at eight o'clock in the morning, leaving at eight o'clock the next day and just looking at the walls the entire time. Some people might like it, but it would drive ninety-five percent of the people on this job absolutely bonkers. As far as the experience now, like I said I only did it for a couple of months, so I really can't give an opinion. Other than knowing you had to do things during the day, whether it was going out for a ride or drilling. I mean you looked forward to going out and getting gas.

Other changes, obviously everything safety wise, but I think being from the old school as opposed to new school, I think the safety issues are not safety issues. I can understand the gloves with the blood, with the diseases etcetera.

Communications should be better. In the city of Newark, it's not what we have available to us in modern technology. Portable radios haven't changed in fifteen years and communications have probably gotten worse. Good old boy hiring, that's gotten worse. Once the operators left civil service and went to political appointees, communications got much worse. Our operators are terrible for the most part. We had professionalism when I first came on. Guys would have light duty jobs and they would know that Six Engine was due at Springfield and Kinney. They know they're right down the corner. As opposed to now an operator doesn't even probably know what's right around the corner there. Doesn't know what a second alarm is. Not too long ago they were sending a company on a tip to go out and check and they weren't even listening to the radio. You're sending a company out to what you think is a fire and then you're not even listening to the radio. You're doing something else on the side. Meanwhile that company calls in, "We have a fire." Acknowledging, send more companies.

They're put there for whatever reason. Different set of standards, political pay back, whatever and they have no knowledge of the fire department. I think communications on our department has really, really gone down. I hate to see any other divisions in the fire department changed in that respect because you lose control.

Discipline has changed. There are a lot of guidelines now that you have to watch, as far as individual discipline. Before it would be nothing if a guy loused up, his company officer would put him on the book, detail him. The Chief would detail the guy. Put a pack on his back was the phrase. Today's times, I don't know if you could even do that because the guy would go to the union and make matters worse. Now they have the Vulcans getting involved. A lot of people want to make things a black white issue, where it's not a black white issue. It has nothing to do with that. The majority of the firemen I know who had a pack on their back were white by about seventy-five percent to twenty-five percent. It had nothing to do with race. It had nothing to do with anything. But now you have to watch anything that you do. As far as individuals, there're rules, laws, unions. Too many people are involved. You can't just say that's it.

But it's a better job than when I came on. Well, no. Let me rephrase that. It was a better job without all the bullshit. I wish you could do twenty-five years if you were with the same people, the same thing, but times have changed. Is it a good job monetary wise? Absolutely, absolutely, it's a good job. I have no regrets. I had a college degree, came on here, have absolutely no regrets about taking the job.

Things have changed so much in society and everything that it can never be the same. You can never go back. There are a lot of things that you can't do that you did before, just for the safety reasons. You can't run into buildings without masks. You can't do this. You can't do that. There are a lot of mandates, but the job itself? No I don't think it's changed that much. Surround yourself with good guys; you'll have a great time.

Ryan: It's probably better to say what the similarities are than it is to talk about changes. Tactics are basically the same. Get to the base of the fire, knock it out, cut it off. That's always been the same. Take control of the stairways. Get the people out. Control the smoke. Those are long standing tenants. That's just the basics of physics that demand you do that.

One of the most distinct changes was going to the Incident Command System, which basically we have used all along without all this formality of specific titles or things. It's been a very clear definition of where you are, what you're doing, and how you're doing it. The biggest change that I've seen is the lack of experience, which only comes from decreased fire, lack of experience that the young people are getting. That's going to be a problem in the future, not now, but it will be. And if you have people who want to be students, they'll learn. There are many books written about it. They'll just have to get into it.

Size of the department, of course, is smaller, but the duties that are being mandated upon us are much more varied. Especially the constraints of wearing this new gear, of the liabilities of responding to haz-mat things, which you're going to be there anyway, so you better know what you're doing. Been a lot of Federal and State laws that have come into effect that we have to obey.

The physics of fighting the fire are always going to be the same. They really are. You can't bring it down to the basics of just saying "Put the wet stuff on the red stuff." because the world has changed, although some people don't know that.

Carter: The job as a whole has less brotherhood than there used to be. The team spirit has shrunk from battalion down to company level where it's existent. And the whole consent decree captains' thing has really cut the heart out of the job. I've seen guys, dedicated dynamos who really don't even want to come to work anymore. So if I had to say the one thing that has most changed the Newark Fire Department, it's the courts of the United States of America that don't care for results. They just want numbers. That's it.

There has always been resistance to change on the fire department, since they've wanted to go with leather buckets in Rome and the guy who the concession for stone buckets didn't want to change. Firemen more than most people, seek the comfort and security of the past. My wife has often said I am an anachronism. I would have been an excellent Jersey City fireman living in the neighborhood, being know as the fireman. Reveling in, glorying in the role of fireman in the neighborhood.

All the major changes are court induced. The demand to create this homogeneous society with no thought to the need for knowledge and intelligence to absorb the skills necessary to do this job. Just numbers for numbers sake has ruined this fire department. If you can learn to live with that and address that, then this still can be a good job. You just have to lower your expectations accordingly. That's the biggest problem. They don't think you need to be smart to do this job.

Langenbach: Things did start to slow down. I attributed that to a lot of things. Remember when you first bought that little calculator that you see for three dollars in the Shop-rite or they give you one if you buy a camera. Those first time calculators were two hundred and fifty dollars. Well, it's the same thing with smoke detectors. Those first ionization smoke detectors were two hundred and fifty dollars. Now in Shop-rite you can get them for five bucks. That helped people. It saved lives. People became more aware of fires. They got them in their incipient stage and they put a bucket of water on them, never called the fire department. You now have probably the fourth generation of people who are getting fire prevention in schools, fire prevention week programs and so forth. I don't think you had those way back when. Now the kids are getting it from the fire department. They're getting it in school. They're getting it on TV. So there's more and more of that.

Connell: The busy companies are still the tightest companies in the city. They always have been, even when I came on the job. All the Down Neck companies below the wall here, everybody was jealous of everybody. It's still that way today. It hasn't changed any. "How come he got this day off and I can't get this day?" Everybody is always watching somebody else.

When you got to the busy companies, nobody really bothered. Nobody cared what the other person did. They had pride in their companies. You'd go to fires and you'd see somebody wrapping a line around a stair post so they could get their line up the stairs faster than the other guy. They'd be having fistfights over the lines. Nobody would give up a hose line. Some of the busy companies, you have some of that mentality left, but the company pride is not here like it used to be. And the closeness of the guys on the job is not like it used to be.

The management of the fire department, unfortunately we've been in a freeze. If anything else we've been going backwards over the last fifteen years. The leadership is not there. We used to be the leader in the state and a good part of the country for firefighting tactics and testing out new equipment. Now they don't even bother calling us anymore because they know the answer is going to be no from the administration. Instead of being a leader, we're a follower now. We're just trying to catch up with everybody else.

The officers, they don't demand respect. I've seen some really, really good officers out there, but most of the officers don't demand the respect the rank requires them to have. They're more worried about covering guys' mistakes in the field than they are in anything else. You just don't have the leadership from the top all the way down. The very top doesn't give the guidance in the direction we're supposed to be going and everybody else is just floundering on the outside. Nobody wants to make a wave. With today's world everybody is afraid to charge somebody because he might be saying he's picking on him because he's Hispanic or he's black or he's Irish or he's Italian or Polish, whatever the case might be. That's a big thing in today's society.

The hours did change, but not for staff personnel. The field got one on, three off, twenty-four hour shifts and we got what we always had. But they just made it official. So instead of working a four day/ten hour week unofficially, we're working a four day/ten hour week officially. A good thing about being Battalion Chief, I get Fridays off

Right now I'm assigned to the Training Academy, but they closed that down. The biggest city in the state kicks us out of our training grounds. They put us in this little office space up here, which is adequate for our needs at the moment, but the firefighting department in the city is going to greatly suffer from the "No place to do drills" and stuff like that. And the city says they're going to build us a new training academy, but it took them six years to build this firehouse and it's still not done.

The transition from Jersey Street to Clinton Avenue was not smooth. It was very rough. The place is still unfinished. We're overrun with rodents here, which made us feel at home because we had the rats down there too.

Langevin: Guys are retiring and they're not being replaced. They don't hire for a long time. That also gets back to the court case. Lists are held up, guys retire, guys are on vacation, this and that. You're down to the bare bones. They continue to cut companies back until they're just barely able to cover the city adequately. I think today, 1999, I think it's still that way. Newark is the largest city in the state of New Jersey and I don't think they have adequate fire protection.

Other changes; the closings of the companies was big. The new way they test the prospective officers. I think those were the two biggest changes. The tactics and the firefighting seemed to remain the same. All in all we have a very, very aggressive firefighting force. That's what makes

Newark's reputation as a fire department excellent, because we're very, very aggressive. We fight fires like no one else on earth as far as I'm concerned.

Perdon: I was always one of those guys who hoped that the job would get progressive in its thinking. I wasn't looking for the world. We used to try and do things to bring the department into the twentieth century. We were, according to the past administration, the fire department. We only fought fires. That's it. The whole world started specializing. You have to do other things. You have to become specialists. Like John Centanni, Jimmy Langenbach, and I tried to get that urban search and rescue unit going. We had everything, the funds in place, the whole nine yards, but then you got the Mickey Mouse jealousies involved in it and it just went by the wayside. Do you know what that would have done for morale for the whole department?

I just don't see enough changes. I mean the changes you see are very Mickey Mouse and they're picayune and in all honesty, it's like it's vindictive. When something comes down from Eighteenth Avenue, it's usually in regards to something that the union did. So, they're going to try to make it a little harder. Like the incident command that came in. It was a pain in the ass, but it was a step in the right direction. Let's become a little progressive. That's the way to think about it. But the whole department never got to a point where personally I wish they would have been. At that time they had the people who would have done it and done a yeoman's job. I mean you had some go-getters. Now, I just don't know if you'll ever see that type again. I mean en mass as we were.

We used to talk at night. We used to think of doing just things that would never cost the city money, but would justify your existence. If you start doing different things, you start justifying your existence. You make it hard for them to cut you back. Unions also, they just never took the bull by the horns and went in that direction. It's not so much the direction that we went in, it's where we didn't go that bothers me.

We haven't been a proactive department at all, not at all. It just seemed like they always want to keep you under thumb. If we did anything to give ourselves any leeway to better justify our existence, they would keep you under thumb. If the police department couldn't do it, if they weren't involved, we couldn't have it at all because there was no way we were going to outshine them. That's me. That's my thinking. Is that how it really is? I don't know. But that's the way it always seemed to me because if they wanted it, they got it. But for us, we always had to be the guy who was kept under thumb and always be the place that if cuts had to be made, they could come here to make cuts. And they could say, "That's all they do. And they're not that busy anymore." We make it easy for them to do it.

Bisogna: Salaries, salary was pretty major. The camaraderie, it's not the way it was. That was more cherished by me over the years than anything. I've been in Ten Truck twelve years. I've had one guy who's been with me the whole time and we're pretty good friends. Several new guys have come and gone because they wanted to go to younger, busier houses, which is great. I like that. You just don't have the same link to people.

And maybe being an officer too. As a fireman you related more with the firemen. When you're the officer, you're the only guy there. Maybe every now and then you'll say something. You'll see the look like, "Well, maybe I don't want to do that." But hey it's my job too. I've got to say we have to do that. I'm not so crazy about doing hydrants, but when that list's got to go in, my name's on it. So, we're going to take a look at the hydrants to make sure they're still in the street. I'm not saying you have to open them all up, but let's go ride around. When it's a warm day and they would rather sit and watch Jerry Springer, I've got to go "Hey, guys why don't we just finish these?" Nobody gives me a hard time, but I'm just making the point that I'm the guy who's got to push you out the door. So, it kind of separates me from the crew a little bit.

And even my friend, who I'll say has been with me forever and is a good friend of mine. When he gets a little pissed off, he'll say "Captain." I'll say, "Uh-oh. Here's something coming. It's not Joe, now. It's 'Wait Cap.'" "Woo, you got a problem here?" Usually he's right, which really sucks.

Ricca: There were a lot more companies down at the Training Academy drilling with us when I came on. And the companies were riding one and five. You had a lot of people helping out to show you what to do.

It seems they're making us change our tactics. They don't want us inside. Go to a fire and see how many times you see the aerial raised. When I first came on, I don't think there was a fire I ever went to that the aerial wasn't up to the building. Even if the building wasn't on fire, it seemed the aerial started to go up. You always had the tiller man from the second due truck company coming up to back you up if you needed something. And a lot of times you look for it. You wanted that second saw because your saw was spent. You don't have that anymore. I've seen times where the whole first due company was on the roof and nobody inside. Now you're looking for a truck man as an engine man, they're all on the roof. We started carrying our own hook at times because of that.

But if there's one thing I have to say it's that, five to ten years will bring the advent of an outside fire department or the tuning fork theory, where if you hit a tuning fork at the right pitch the fire will go out. Maybe that will happen before any other changes.

Chapter Five: Changing Technology

Fredette: All the companies got the inch and a half hose, but I would say it was in the '60s before they depended so much on it. Before that it was the booster and the two and a half. Suddenly they figured that stretching two and a half was a lot of trouble, so they used the inch and a half. They also had a three-inch suction hose. Now I got out in February of '73. I was sixty-five.

Vetrini: I think the equipment was always changing. We were getting different fog tips. Then they were getting special tips to put onto the aerial. They had those high-pressure fog guns. Fourteen Engine had it. There were always some changes. Our own clothing changed. Our helmets changed. The masks changed. I missed the MSA filter mask, the Burrell. I always felt that it was so easy, but they contended some lives were lost in using it. But if I felt it getting tight, I would get out. You would tell the guy "I have to leave." They came in with the hose that didn't have to hang. They started to bring that out to the busier companies first. Then we had the change of apparatus. We had the side-saddle, the bucket seats, nobody riding on the back step. But the riots brought that on, too. They brought in the diesels.

Redden: Communications changed tremendously. Through the use of radio we were able to operate much more efficiently on the fire ground. Protection for the men, self-contained breathing apparatus, better helmets; although it was a sacrilege to lose your leather helmet. In spite of the fact that some of them didn't like Nomex and other material like Nomex, I think they were a great advance in protecting men at fires. They've added Snorkels, Squirts, things like this to the types of apparatus.

Kinnear: Communications, going from no radios to walkie-talkies. I think if I had to pick out one thing as far as firefighting was concerned, that would be the biggest thing. Because basically, changing to inch and a half made a difference, but that was a change that didn't change your system. It just made stretching line a little easier, a faster interior attack. But communications, when that changed, that changed everything. From being tied to the house to being able to roam, see your district, do building inspection and hydrant inspections.

Going to the use of masks and then going to air masks. I think that's been a big thing, as far as protecting the guys' lives. I think we didn't realize when we came on. We were supposedly iron men; go in and take the smoke, part of the job that's all. We went to the filter masks. We realized we couldn't go into a cellar or something, but you never realized that maybe stuff is coming through that filter. Maybe it's not as good as you think. Going to the air mask was definitely an improvement. Equipment naturally has been upgraded, but it hasn't really basically changed that much. A pumper is still a pumper; a ladder is still a ladder.

Clothing has improved, of course, naturally in the last couple of years. I think that's a great thing because we wore rubber coats; and they were rubber coats. If you got too close to a fire, the coat could melt onto you. It never happened fortunately because using a two and a half you never got that close where it got hot. Like today, you get right into the fire. I imagine if you had a rubber coat on today and you got close, it might adhere to you.

F. Grehl: The equipment kept improving to make for greater efficiency. When we first went on, it was either a booster or a two and a half inch hose. Then somewhere in the early '50s we went to inch and a half. These are the improvements, but no matter what you do, you still have to put water on the fire in excess of the BTUs it's creating in order to put the fire out. You just have better equipment to do it. I think training was a little better, too. When I first came on, we were basically trained by our captain. Your company officer trained you at a fire. How and what you're going to do, under what conditions, and so on. What impressed me is we were an inside fire department. What you can do inside with a couple of good lines. Of course, it was a lot harder when the only line you had was a two and a half and you had to drag it up two, three flights of stairs. It was a lot harder to maneuver, get around the corners, and go from one room to the other room.

Apparatus improved tremendously. It works easier. The pumps back in the old days were what they call positive displacement piston type pumps, the old Ahrens Foxx. They got into the centrifugal pumps with those LaFrances when they came. Very confusing because they had to be primed and the old timers were tough. Nobody's going to accept anything new out there. "I've been doing this for fifty years and this is the best way." It took a while to get them acclimated to priming pumps and the tricks of priming it.

When I first came on there were no radios. The only ones who had radios were the Chief's cars. Of course there were no radios for individual companies. No portable radios. The radios in the cars were in the car. That's what you used. Then they put them in all companies. Today companies have portable radios. They're tremendous. You can do an awful lot. One of the things that shows people don't appreciate radios is a fire we had over on Chadwick Avenue. En route I could see the thing was going good, two or three homes. I sent a second alarm from the car. When I got out of the car, I have to start directing these companies. I can't have them all come in from Avon Avenue. I stood in the middle of the street with my uniform cap on. I didn't have rubber goods on and I had a radio in my hand.

I directed the companies where to go. Once we had things settled, I put my rubber goods on and continued my job.

Well, the next first day in I got called to City Hall. Caufield had us there. It seemed the neighborhood group, community group, had complained about the guy in the white hat who stood in the middle of the street and did nothing. So, I says to the Director, "You have to be kidding." It was a woman who was the spokesperson. "You have to be kidding. Don't you explain to her what I do at a fire? Don't you explain to her about a command post and it's my job out in front of the building?" "Well, she seems to think you did nothing." I said, "Wait, before we go any further. Call upstairs and get a tape down from the fire." So, we got the tape down and we played it for them. Well, of course she heard that I had sent for a second alarm before I even got there. Then she heard all the radio talk about assigning companies. I said, "Lady, that's my job. That's what my job is to do. My job is not to pick up a hose or anything else. My job is to make sure they all coordinate." But that's what happens when the public sees you doing nothing. They think you're doing nothing. Radio, radio's what did it. What we do otherwise. "Freddie, go up to the corner and tell the company when it gets in. Go up to the other corner and get this company and tell them what you want." Or the company would stop at the corner and the captain would run down and say, "Chief, what do you want me to do?" That was again without radios. That's five minutes time that you save.

At one test, they asked me an oral question, "What are the two biggest changes on the fire department that you have seen up to date?" My answer was inch and a half hose and radio. They were apparently satisfied because they gave me a ninety. They were the two biggest changes. Getting away from dragging two and a half every place you go. Being able to do the job with fewer men and being able to move people, direct them, and take care of their safety.

When you stretch two and a half inch, you need a little more men. You can stretch an inch and a half with two guys. But you stretch a two and a half you need three, depending on how high you're going. You just can't have one guy in the stairwell, another guy on the nozzle with a little excess hose with a two and a half. You need people all over the place. One of the things we did with two and a half that became a problem was on a stairwell we would go up and try to feed it up that way, but it was very, very heavy when charged. Basically we were taught to lay it on the stairs because it took away from that excess weight. One of the training things we had later was to put a hose strap underneath a coupling and wrap it around a railing to take the weight off of it. When we got the inch and a half we could do the same thing. Stretch it up the stairwell, but the weight wasn't there. Hose straps are very rarely used today, but they were mandatory years back.

Unfortunately, there's no way we can change the basics because the most economical method we have of putting out fires is water. In order to give the water, we have the same basic principles. We try to improve the equipment to reduce the friction loss so you have better pressure, better volume, things of that nature. Inch and three quarter hose today with the proper pressure, with rapid water gives you as much water as two and a half inch hose. That's a tremendous improvement. Two guys can do it if need be. There was a budget savings there. Another reason we didn't need one and five and ride a lot of times one and two is the fellows could do the job. That was the important thing. It didn't make any difference how many people you had. They always seemed to do the job. They gave that little extra. The job always managed to get done. When you get to the administration, they say "Hey they're still doing it with less people."

McCormack: There've been major, major changes. Because inch and a half line did more than the booster did, but it did almost as much as the two and a half inch line. Over a period of time it influenced manpower because prior to that when you operated a charged two and a half inch line in a building you needed four, six, eight, ten men to move that line even a couple of rooms. You had to lighten up all the way on that line. You had to drag it. With an inch and a half line, two or three men could do more work than ten men with a two and a half inch line. They could do it better, more efficiently. That was the start of the manpower change because it was more efficient. Less people could do as much or more work with that line. The second major change was the masks, the self-contained masks. Before that we wouldn't wear masks. They were inefficient to start with and we wouldn't bother to wear them most of the time. It was frowned upon to wear a mask. You got the line in and held the fire until the squad got there. They were the mask specialists. They'd take over your line and put the fire out if they could. Now with the self-contained masks you have a much more aggressive fire department, a much more efficient fire department. They go right in with their masks, with their small diameter lines, go right to the seat of the fire, knock it down. They get a fast knock down in a couple of minutes. It's a much more efficient operation than it was before.

Safety consciousness came about in the '70s, when they started all those regulations. Nobody is against safety. I'm not against safety. These men deserve all the protection they can get. I've got a son on the job. I certainly want him to get the best protection he can get. I'm not really against safety. I really don't want to criticize things, but I look at things like those leather fire helmets that we bought when we came on the job. Firemen wore those for generations. I wore them for twenty, twenty-five years before they changed to the plastic helmets. In all those years, I never remember any firefighter ever suffering a severe head injury. I know a few guys who were hit on the head with those helmets on. Pieces of wood or something like that fell off a building. They might have possibly been knocked a little dizzy, but I don't ever remember anyone receiving a severe head injury wearing those helmets. When they changed them over to plastics, we were told they did tests on those helmets and that if you dropped a one inch steel ball from a hundred feet up or whatever, it would penetrate these helmets, where the plastic wouldn't do that. We were also told the leather, being natural material, would absorb moisture. The more moisture the helmet absorbed, the more electrically conductive it became. So you could suffer an electrical shock through your helmet and get injured that way. Well, technically, maybe that is a true statement. Maybe you could prove that in a laboratory. But in reality I never heard of a fireman getting an electrical shock through any kind of helmet.

The biggest advantage to the plastic helmet they're wearing today is maintenance. The leather helmets required an awful lot of maintenance, where these plastic helmets today need practically no maintenance. You don't have to paint them. You don't have to do anything with them. In that sense, I think the plastic helmet is an improvement. But as far as being safer, I put very little credence in that.

Masterson: You went from the aerial ladder to the bucket. You went from the two and a half inch to the inch and a half hose. Those are the things you work with and realize because you're using them. After I made that rescue on Emmet Street, all the engines got thirty-five foot extension ladders. Before that the only thing they had was twenty foot ladders. They were no good for the third floor. They wouldn't reach it right. I was just looking to make that grab, but then after that we all got thirty-five foot extension ladders on the engines, two sections. Because they couldn't put a big one on, they had to have two sections because the engines had no room to carry it.

Freeman: Hose, the supply hose has gone from two and a half to three inch to four inch. We got rid of the three-inch and the Smith valve. That was very complicated for a lot of guys. If you didn't use it, you forgot how to use it. We're down to just a plain hydrant, four inch to a hydrant. Now they have the hose that has the smooth lining, the inch and three quarters. We have the two-inch hose, which is very difficult to use. We're the only company in the city to try that and the only tour that liked it was the third tour. They say it's easy to use. Yes, if you have a full crew, one and four. Even if you have a full crew, you're going to need at least three or four guys to hump that hose up to the next floor. That's almost like moving a two and half. That's a lot of water. The nozzle is great. You have plenty of water. You don't have to use that much pressure with that nozzle, but the hose is not mobile. You can't bend that hose around corners. You stick it into a room? No way. It's just so heavy. You can take it all the way up to the third floor and once you get it there you can wet the hose and use it. What if you have to move that hose down the hall and try to get more hose if you don't have enough? That's tough. Try to move a two and half like that, up to the next floor if you don't have enough men. Right now; everybody's riding light. As an outside line fine, you use it just like you use a two and a half between buildings maybe or if you have a big conflagration. But as an inside line no.

Now they have the smooth lined hose where you don't have to use that much pressure. You have less friction loss. So where you pumped before at a hundred and sixty pounds, a hundred and seventy pounds, now you can pump at a hundred and fifty and you get the same water with less pressure.

Six Engine used that hose at a fire in a two story industrial building. When they wet the line this guy came flying off the porch, off the steps into the street hanging onto that hose. They had given him too much pressure. He was lying on the ground there because they forgot to adjust the pressure. They gave him too much pressure when he opened the line. The chief said that they were going to give us that hose on our new apparatus. So the equipment that they're coming out with is really good.

Masks, like the positive pressure masks we just recently got here, excellent. Before you had demand type masks. Sometimes if you had a leak or if the connection was loose you'd be inhaling smoke. You didn't know where it was coming from. When you're in that kind of environment and you don't know where it's coming from, you try to tighten things up and you're still not doing it. It could be coming in from the edge of your mask. With the positive pressure, it's perfect.

I think the turn out gear is better. We went from leather helmets to polycarbonate. We went from rubber coats to Nomex. We went from just a plain leather working gloves to that glove we have to use now. If any of the equipment goes bad we can always exchange it for a new piece of equipment. They get new apparatus every seven years, every eight years. That way it's better. The equipment is better, better apparatus.

McGee: The equipment always got better gradually. They went to better deck guns, better nozzles on the deck guns, fog nozzles. All this equipment made it possible to put a lot more water on a fire, which contained a lot of fires. That was one of the changes. Equipment was a big change. I think that's one of the reasons they were able to get away with running with fewer men, even though I don't recommend it at all. They were able to do it without too much flak because they did have all this better equipment. Also the size of the supply hose for water increased from two and a half to three-inch to four-inch. Now I think they even have something bigger that we didn't have. You're literally bringing the hydrant right in front of the building. You could feed four engine companies off your engine company. In that sense, dramatic changes happened in terms of equipment, in terms of the ability to put all your eggs closer to the fire. Before you had fifteen companies coming into the street, it changed in the sense that you could park your apparatus and go. As long as you could see the first due engine had a feed. Or maybe another company had a feed from the other direction and he's hooked up. You could almost walk down to the fire with your cart, hook up to the company that was in front of the building, and go in, which made it a lot easier. That's a very important change I would say.

McGrory: Equipment wise all fire departments were starting to evolve and starting to change, quick couplings and stuff that the Germans had so damn long ago it's ridiculous. In the last number of years, we're just finding out about it. The Navy used inch and a half hose for years and years before we found out about it. Cotton jacketed, double cotton jacket rubber lined hose we had to hang after every fire. You had to wash it off and clean it.

But the equipment got better. It wasn't a violent departure. It was slow progression of the equipment getting better. I don't think they have any fox hooks left, but the fox hooks. The Halligan came and John Higginson came up with the idea of putting a knob on the bottom. What a job we had getting that knob put on. The Halligan didn't slip out of your hand and you could use that knob as a battering tool. It was a great idea.

The advancement of the inch and half pre-connected and the reliance on it. Going to inch and three quarter; going to pre-connected deck guns; going to different types of aerial ladders. Self-contained masks allowed us to get in very good. Get in and hit the fire close. You could get in closer to the fire than you could with the old Burrells. But sometimes that can work against you. You get so close you get too close. Still in all, if you're doing all your equipment right, you're going to do a better job. But there are pro's and con's. There are pluses and minuses. You get a mask like the mask they use today. What's it thirty pounds more on your back? The coats weigh more. Newark is going to have to go to bunker pants. That's going to weigh down more. They should get rid of boots and go to the shoe, the eight, ten inch boot instead of the rubber boot. The constant flow nozzles were a big help because you could know how much time you had. We were using our own Mattydales before the apparatus came with them.

Denvir: Switching from the Burrell to the demand mask was a pretty good change. That made a change in the operations. The Squirt was a good idea. Not the one that they had later, the first ones they got were good. Nine Engine's was on a Ward LaFrance. In Eighteen, we got the one that was on the Henderson chassis. It didn't have any shock absorbers in the system, just shook itself apart, but the nozzle was good. Then they went to Emergency One. The boom was slow. Where the other ones you could get it up real quick and do a job with it. Put a lot of fires out without going in the building with that. I thought it was good in its place. It wasn't a cure all for everything, but in its place it was good.

Freda: When I first came on the job in 1959, the Rescue Squad were the only ones to have self-contained breathing apparatus. Everyone had the canister type masks. Before that, even going back before that, no one had masks period, but the Rescue Squad. In the '50s, people had the canisters, but they didn't have self-contained.

Like I said, when the canister type masks came in, the Rescue Squad was the only unit that had self- contained breathing apparatus. Not the self-contained breathing apparatus you know today. It was called a Chemox canister mask. It was developed by the Navy and was nothing more than a canister that you inserted into the mask. The moisture in your breath would start the mask off. You actually had to breathe into it so the moisture in your breath would activate the chemical in the canister, which produced oxygen. They were very long lasting masks. They would last an hour and later on I remember in the Squad, they had a two- hour canister. If you got into a situation that was below grade or a ship fire, then the Rescue Squad would come, take the line off of you, and fight the fire. Then gradually everyone in the city was given self-contained apparatus and the Rescue Squad lost that.

Smith: What they're doing today is reducing the effectiveness of a fireman by encapsulating him in bunker gear. He can't do anything. Today, I get the impression that they're trying to protect the firemen to a point where he's ineffective. You can't encapsulate him in a concrete blockhouse and expect him to have agility and mobility. It can't be done. It's an inherently dangerous job. There are certain risk factors that you have to take. Calculated risk is part of your job.

Dunn: The biggest change I've seen in the fire service was going from the filtered type of mask to the self-contained breathing apparatus that we're using today. It allows us to safely do our job in a much more professional manner. The filter mask was a health hazard to us. We just weren't aware. It allowed us to go where we didn't belong, where we were breathing in products of combustion that we shouldn't be breathing in. The self-contained breathing apparatus was adopted by the fire service. Our people are very comfortable with it and they trust it. That's very important. We trust our masks ninety-nine point nine percent to be effective. And that has allowed us to perform our job in a much safer manner from our own point of view and allowed us to do a better job for the citizens.

Carragher: Changes in the fire service, the masks, going from the air filter mask to the Scott air-pack was a tremendous factor. What has enhanced it a lot more now is the lighter tank. Originally we were up around forty pounds with a mask on. Now, what are they, fifteen or sixteen? I think that difference there is tremendous.

The inch and three quarter hose is a tremendous thing today. When you can make an attack line with inch and three quarter and get nearly as much water with it as we used to get out of a two and a half with one or two men doing it. That's a tremendous factor. The four-inch hose for the feeds, we had always had a problem getting water. Now we have four-inch hose. Companies bring in their own feeds in most cases. You're not losing too much from friction loss either. You're getting pretty good water.

The apparatus, the Squirts are a tremendous tool. If they were maintained correctly and used right, it's a valuable tool, especially with less manpower. If you had a couple of buildings going, you put these in the right spot, you can knock down fire that maybe it would take two or three companies to do before. Aerial ladders, we have aerial ladders that are slightly longer, so you have more reach. The elimination of the tiller cab was a big change in the truck companies. Now you only have one man responsible for the truck instead of two. Pumpers, twelve hundred and fifty gallon pumpers are coming in now. Everybody carries five hundred gallons of water. Twenty-Seven and Nineteen have seven hundred and fifty gallons. What a tremendous potential to go to work with.

Changing to the aluminum ladders instead of wood gave you less breakage. Automatic transmissions in the apparatus, radios, walkie-talkies are getting better. If you're fortunate enough to get one of the newer walkie-talkies, it's probably one of the better ones we've had since I came on the job. The one thing I'd like to see is the alarm system updated. Our alarm system is still the 1900 system here. They built the firehouse in what, 1900 and we still have the same alarm system here.

Cahill: I think some of the apparatus have gotten better. I really have nothing to base this on, just the fact that you don't see breakdowns and apparatus out of service like you used to see. After they phased the Macks out, they brought in a whole variety of stuff. There was no continuity at all. Six Engine had one particular piece. Then the city would buy five others. I don't know if that was a result of bidding or what. Now you seem to be getting more standardized. It seemed to be we went through a whole period there with a mish-mash of different types. Then just for your own health, going from Burrells to the SCBAs was a tremendous change.

Butler: The upgrade in equipment that's something that I think is very beneficial too. You're looking at the good side, the upgrade in apparatus. The actual motor vehicle apparatus, the turn out gear the firemen are wearing, the breathing apparatus, it's one touch with life safety that they really need in order to do the job right.

Cody: Everyone has their own face piece for the mask. The apparatus is much improved where now they carry five hundred or seven hundred and fifty gallons of water. We were carrying one fifty and three hundred. The hose is bigger, four inch hose. I never even worked with four-inch hose as a captain. It was a little bit of an adjustment for me, coming over here as a Battalion Chief to tell people what to do with four inch hose because I never worked with it. I could tell you to drop two lines, a two and a half and a three from a hydrant or something like that, but to get used to taking the hydrant into the block with you by using the four-inch hose, it was an experience for me. They've improved the apparatus quite a bit.

Wargo: The apparatus has been kept up the last ten years or so. They started a program of replacing the apparatus. We do have good apparatus right now. The only problem is we don't have spares. If anything is wrong with the engine or the truck, the spares they are driving are in very bad shape. They're not really dependable.

The equipment has changed for the better. There are pros and cons on the ladder pipes being on the end of the aerial. People say you should be able to operate with them no matter where they are, but I don't think it's a good idea here. I think they're going to break them. In training you can line up the ladder the way you want it. At a fire you can't. You just can't see what you're doing.

McGovern: The gear has changed. It's all for the better in the long run. It's going to keep these guys on the job now alive longer. It's rare that guys get ten, fifteen years out of retirement now. Where maybe in the future maybe they'll get thirty years and it's all because of this. That's one of the changes I see. We used to just do what you have to do. No matter what it took. Now you can't do it because it's not safe. It's affecting the outcome, but in the long run guys are living longer for it.

The Sqaud was a good place to see the changes because they used to give all the new stuff to the Squad to test. That was a good reason for being in the Squad. You got a lot of the new innovations. Of course, they didn't buy anything, but they let you test it. The big innovation was when they came up with the lightweight aluminum tanks. That made a big difference. Getting in and out of windows, climbing ladders, they were just a few pounds and the size alone was smaller. Probably twenty years from now they'll have something you can put in your pocket.

What they do have to do now is get everybody these PASS alarms. Guys just don't remember to turn them on. You need something that has to be built into the mask or something you can't mess with. It goes on when you go on. You have so much on your mind when you get there.

Prachar: The apparatus have been getting newer and bigger. Other changes, it's hard to say. A lot of people don't like changes. Tools, tools are getting better as far as the truck company, with your Halligans and stuff like that. We always had wooden pike poles breaking. You tried to do the job; you couldn't because a pole would snap. Tools? You couldn't ask for some of the better tools. Rescue, the tools they carry on there. The Rabbit Tool, fantastic piece of equipment, jaws fantastic if you know how to use it. You need the knowledge to use it. If you don't have the knowledge, don't touch it. The Rabbit Tool, go up to the projects, what an improvement, I would have loved the Rabbit Tool when I was in Five Truck twenty years ago. Instead of carrying the maul and the battering ram, here you go up with a small piece of hydraulic equipment. The door's open in two seconds.

Great improvements, great improvements but it's not like your old time fire department. You figure three or four times a night walking up the stairs in the projects with the battering ram, the maul, your mask and everything.

Now you carry a little satchel. We're in the apartment in two seconds. Where you used to be ten minutes with the maul and the ram depending on how many locks they had on the door. I love the equipment now. Give me a good piece of equipment, an aerial that goes up quick. Remember now you have everything hydraulic. Your aerial, one lever and out come your outriggers, the truck is up in the air, you put your aerial up. Back then you had to pull a pin, pull the outriggers out, screw them down, set them up. It's time consuming.

When I was in Rescue, one of the main things we started there was carrying two K-12 saws. Everybody said, "Why two K-12s?" One had a wooden blade, one with a metal blade. If you had a K-12 in a truck company with the wooden blade on and you had to use the metal blade, you had to sit there and change the blade. Now they all have two saws. Take off, boom, boom with your roll down doors and everything. Everybody's right in there, everybody fights the fire, you go home. Sure equipment, great improvement, fire apparatus along with your tools.

Finucan: Technically, there were no big changes. I could name the technical changes we had. We were issued portable radios. We went to synthetic hose so you don't have to hang it. We went from canister masks to SCBA, to a lighter SCBA, to a positive pressure SCBA, just little changes along the same direction, the lighter masks, the Mark IVs they have out there with the tanks. I was always a light weigh. When I came on the job, I was like a hundred and forty five pounds most of my career. Now I'm up to like one fifty-five, so the masks were heavy to me. I was always in good shape, but the mask was always a problem for me. When we got the new tanks I felt like superman. It was such a difference to me because the tanks were like fifteen pounds lighter.

McDonnell: There have been changes in the apparatus, some for good, some for bad. The gear, I think is horrible today. What they make them wear today. I think it's totally inappropriate. Bunker gear, there's nothing wrong with it in December or January, but no way a fireman should be wearing bunker gear, no way in hell where you have a hundred degree temperature change that you should be wearing the same equipment in August that you wear in January.

The rigs, I wouldn't say they're any better or any worse. It's probably a tradeoff; things that you lost as opposed to a lot of things that you gained. Actually there hasn't been any real major change in equipment, in apparatus since I've been on the job. It's changed in a lot of ways, but it's no major improvement and really no major decline. They both have their good points. You give up one thing, you get something else.

Pianka: Over the years they've given you more protective equipment. They encapsulated you and they've given you fresh air to breath. They've given you the ability to go further and people are stumbling into situations where they shouldn't be. We switched over to this new equipment. There's two ways of looking at this stuff. In certain ways it encapsulates you. It's hotter. It's more difficult in certain ways. The adjustment process was the toughest. You felt you were confined. But in time, like everything else on this fire department, you learned to adapt and you learned to live with it and you look at the good parts of it.

There are some very important good parts to the new equipment. Just takes you a while to realize what it is. During the winter you're much warmer. It gives you much better protection. There is something to this whole concept of being totally enclosed because water was always coming underneath the old coats or if you had fire or anything it could be lapping at your butt. I don't know. I think I adapted to it just like everybody else did.

I remember once working outside on a roof with the old Midwestern coat. I had to take it off because I literally felt like I was getting sunburned through it. It sounds stupid, but the thing got so hot on my back that it was burning me through the coat. That shows you it didn't give you that much protection. It didn't do anything for you really. I don't think it did. These coats hold up better. Between Five Truck and my early years at Six Engine, I bet you I went through five coats, at least four or five coats because they would leak through the seams inside. They would buckle up. They didn't hold up. Where as, I've been wearing this outfit I have now for a number of years. Sure it shows some wear and tear, but it holds up relatively well. Okay, granted maybe I went to more fires then, but these things hold up a lot better.

I don't wear the hoods and I don't know a guy who does. I don't know what's going to happen. Like I said, I can adapt. It may take a while, but I'll adapt. These hoods though, aren't going to make it. I see the theory behind it. The problem is in the implementation. They're very difficult to get on. When you get to a fire, things have to be easily put on. You can't be fumbling with it because guys won't use it. You're pumped up. You know there's a fire there. You're trying to get out as quick as you can. You're already worried about putting your mask on and stuff like that and how you're going to get to the fire. You have to drop everything. You have to take your gloves off because you can't put these things on with your gloves. It's impossible. You have to take your gloves off, put this thing on, adjust it, play with it; then put on your helmet. Guys aren't going to do that. Guys refuse to do that.

They use the other excuse. Well, it's just too much. We don't have our ears to use as a guide. Eh, maybe. You know the old theory if it's too hot, your ears will tell you. Possible, I can get by with that so far. I feel too enclosed. Eh, maybe. That's not the reason. The reason it isn't going to work is it just takes too much fumbling with it. You have to put your mask on, then you have to put this thing over it. It's hard to do. Nobody's using them. I don't use it. I did it once at a fire. I said, "You've got to be kidding me. Forget it." Put it in my pocket, same thing with all the guys here, all the guys, almost everybody in the field. There're a few guys who have them. I don't see who the hell wears them. Nobody wears them. It's impossible. In theory it's a good idea. You're right, you can get burnt pretty seriously around your ears and neck, but you can get burnt even worse with these things.

Rotonda: Some of the equipment is much better. I mean, I wouldn't say the durability of the trucks, but I would say some of the equipment that we use. Like the K-12 saw I think is great compared to when we tried to use chain saws. But yet the chain saw was better than the axe. I mean only in the movies you see the fireman with the axe. It looks great. See how it is trying to open up a roof or something like that. Forget about it. And the maul is a very good instrument too. Break it down. But people don't know why you break it down, do all this destruction, about gases and stuff. They don't understand it.

T. Grehl: You have to have a better mask where it's not a demand anymore. It's a positive pressure to keep the smoke out. But we missed the whole tradition of the fire department. The boots that we used to have and the coats, it's not as protective, but I'll go on record. I'll never wear a hood.

I never wore a hood because I know Mike Petrone in my heart would have been dead if he had his hood on and he's still alive today. So, I think we went overboard with certain protections, certain mandates for that.

The pre-connected hoses are probably one of the best things that ever happened, the Mattydales. When I came on you never had pre-connected hose. You had to take the time and hook up. It's amazing how fast lines get stretched and water goes on the fire. My father told me stories of when nobody ever used the booster tank. Years ago, before I came on. Nobody ever used a pre-connected with a booster tank. It's amazing how much fire you can put out in thirty seconds if you get everything working, as opposed to a delay of thirty seconds or a minute. Everything being lighter is obviously a big plus, the ladders, aluminum ladders as opposed to the wooden forty-five footers or forty footers.

Turn out gear, now it's heavier. It's going to kill somebody. There's no doubt in my mind. Whether it's heart attack or because we have better protection to go deeper into the building and last longer, something's got to give. Once your adrenalin stops and everything backs down and you have heat exhaustion from this forty-five pound plus you're carrying.

We just measured what a fireman goes in with. I forget what it was. It's astronomical. Carry a port-a-lite. Carry a tank. Carry a radio. Carry everything else. Your body's not meant to do that. If you're ten pounds overweight normally, you could feel the difference in the summer. Just throw an extra sixty pounds of garbage on you. You're not meant to work more than a minute or two and we're being put into extreme conditions. So, yes we helped our self for the safety. We can go deeper into the building, but somebody's going to die from the heat exhaustion and all that stuff.

Ryan: Types of apparatus, types of gear we wear, types of breathing apparatus have all changed. Different gear? Yes, we have some new toys that we play with, that we've gotten and they've been very beneficial. The infa-red camera for one is really good.

Carter: I still wear a leather helmet even though it's OSHA compliant and NFPA compliant. I still wear a leather helmet. I don't want a yellow coat. Firemen don't wear yellow coats. I had state of the art black with yellow trim. Light-weight, very expensive, bought it myself, but I still looked like a fireman. Now they have us riding on these DPW yellow trucks because of that Solomon up in New York State. Fire trucks are red. That's just the way it is. But we do have to change. I'm in the forefront of change, but change in a rational, necessary manner. Unlike many firemen who if they could still wear black rubber coats and leather helmets without any inside and boots and no gloves they'd do it. So I want to see change not for the sake of change, but to address specific, demonstrable needs. But the fire service as whole revels in the past, hundreds of years of tradition and unimpeded by progress.

Connell: The equipment? It's a lot better. The first mask we had was great for its time and age. The problem was we were taught not to use them. Now, everybody in the Academy including myself encourages people to use them as long and as much as possible. The type of fires we have now. The fires today are hotter. They're smokier. There are more toxic gases in them due to plastics. When we had a house fire almost everything in the house was natural materials. There might be a little piece of garbage from Japan someplace, a token somewhere, but most of the stuff was natural materials. Horse hair mattresses, furniture was actually made out of wood and natural fabrics. Today everything is plastic, rayon, orlon. They burn a lot hotter. Burn a lot smokier. This one job in Seven Truck was made a signal eleven and we tore open the house, tore it all apart. The smoke condition in the house was unbelievable. They had a plastic organ that caught fire and burned. It gave off this large amount of heat and smoke on the second floor, but actually there was very little fire damage.

The guys are better equipped with the masks they have, the positive pressure masks, but they're faced with a lot more hazards than we were. They have synthetic materials. The building construction now is dangerous. When I first came on all the houses in Newark were made with two by six, two by eights, two by tens, two by twelves, two by fours. Today everything is metal frame, prefab, synthetic boards, pressboards. Again they're using chemicals and glues to glue all these pieces of wood together. You haven't got the strength. Right now the average truss roof, new house they're building down here, has a five year life expectancy. There were fires in houses in Newark I've been into five, six, seven times before it finally became just a basement. So, the guys have a whole new problem facing them.

With the new turn out gear you're fully encapsulated. Hoods at the moment are an option in the state. I understand they're going to become mandatory very shortly. I never liked hoods. When I was broken in, your ears were your thermometers. I still believe that. We're too overly protected now. We're getting ourselves into problems, into temperatures and places we shouldn't be. We're not paying attention to the warning signs the buildings are giving us. There was a program on television a couple days ago about the turnout gear we're wearing now and how guys are actually getting pouched inside their turnout gear. They're coming out with special computers for putting inside your lining to let you know when you're in a position you shouldn't be in so you can get out before you actually get hurt.

The fire department has always been resistant to change and right now I'm one of the dinosaurs of the fire department. And my views are compared to way back when. But then too I used to think it was fun to suck in the orange and green and purple from dump fires I was fighting. If it was up to me, I'd put on my three quarter length boots and my longer coat for truck operations, but definitely not a hood. I was more comfortable in that, but the new gear is very good in the winter times. I give it that. They are nice in the winter. The rest of the time they suck.

Pignato: One of the biggest changes I saw was truck companies getting radios. When I was a captain at Five Truck, I didn't have a radio. I had a scanner. I bought a scanner so I could tell what was going on when I had my men climbing up into a high rise or into the projects. The engine's often there first. You're coming from another area. We never knew what was going on. You're working up on a roof and you had no way of contacting anybody down below. All the time you're still on the roof. You'd throw something down to get their attention.

Radios back then would have saved a lot of problems because you could have radioed the chief and told him what was going on. You could see things from up there that guys down on the ground can't see; if there's something dangerous, the extension of the fire, or whatever. You had to yell or climb down the ladder to tell him what was going on. So radios were probably one of the biggest things.

The rest of the equipment, I think all sucks. The gloves suck. The boots I find are a little better. Only because they're short and I had Nomex turn out pants when I first came on the job. These coats are not very comfortable. The pants, they just make you over heated. These shirts, the Nomex work uniform is very hot. It's counterproductive to a good fireman's wellbeing. I think. If it makes you hot, you can't perform. It cuts your time in half. How much work you can do? What the hell's the point of it? It's okay if you're just standing out in the middle of the street, throwing water from the street, but not if you're actually doing something.

Bisogna: I don't know about major changes. When I came on they still had Burrell's hanging on the hooks, but nobody used them. I mean the filters or whatever they were, the oxygen generators. They had them in the Academy. Showed us how they worked, Chemoxs. We had air cylinders, the old kind. Before us they weren't positive pressure. You had to break the seal. When you inhaled, you opened the valve on the mask. That was a little telling on your lungs. You had to overcome that valve every time you took a breath. They were a little hard. When they went to positive pressure, which was pretty good, that took a lot of the load off.

Other major changes were they got rid of the tiller cabs. They got the new gear, which I don't like, better masks. Automatic transmissions, the trucks are better. I always liked truck work and the trucks work a lot nicer, the automatic jacks. They're a lot stronger than they were. The ladders are a lot stronger. I feel a lot more confident working off of one, where the older ones were swaying in the breeze a little bit. You had to be careful if you had a ladder pipe up there. If you were operating any kind of line off them, they were a little frailer. So the equipment seems better, but it doesn't hold up as long. Like an old Mack would last twenty-five years. These new rigs are falling apart after five and seven. I don't know about major changes. It's been all gradual stuff.

Ricca: The helmets had just changed from the leather to the plastic right around the time I was appointed. I had a plastic helmet. The guys with the leather helmets, they'd look at the thing like it was an animal in a cage, wondering what the heck it was. Then you had to buy your own stuff, too. Everything was out of pocket.

The Squirts and the big hose will bring about an outside fire department. I think that's what it's all designed for. We're going to pull up to a building in the future and we're going to open up our big hose lines and we're going to surround and drown everything. Because of the equipment they're giving us, they're stymieing us. The boom of the Squirt coming up to hit the third floor of a building and you're on the second floor. Guys aren't going to take too much of that. Eighteen Engine one time on Belmont Avenue, I'll never forget it, I was driving the rig and Pete was tillering. We went up on the side walk and took the roof. We were up there with Chief Smith, Captain Killeen. The boom of the Squirt came up and it was like a one eyed monster coming up. It started washing us off. Well, Frank McCrone fell on Kevin Killeen and I laid on Jimmy Smith. Kevin was screaming on the air, "Shut that Squirt! Shut that Squirt!" Chief Smith said to me, "Next time let me get washed off the roof." because I broke every bone in his body when I jumped on him.

Chapter Six: Changing Generations

Fredette: Today, you're getting a lot of young guys where we got older men. There were quite a few college men who came on our job. Like Captain Cawley, he passed the BAR examination. He was a lawyer. Back in '38 there were no jobs or the jobs didn't pay. If a college man got a job, he made eighteen dollars a week. So, they got older men. Now you're getting kids coming in at twenty-one, twenty-two years of age.

Kinnear: There was a much tighter semi-military structure than there is today. I don't know where we got away from that. The captain was boss. You didn't call him Joe or Sam or Bill or something. You called him captain. If he'd say snap to, you'd snap to. If he said "You've got the second floor today." You went up and you did a good job on the second floor. The Battalion Chief would come around the same as he does today, but I had worked with a Battalion Chief for so long at Six Engine we had a little more loose relationship with the Battalion Chief than the other companies. When he came around to the companies they lined up and he read them the orders and things like that. When you heard the Deputy was coming or when he said something, you really stood to, if you could. He was a semi-god. It was very different than it is today.

Some of the change is good, I mean some things were too strict, I think, but today it's gone the other way. It's gotten too loose. We lost discipline somewhere along the line. Guys now can get away with a lot. Guys got away with stuff in my day too. Drinking and things like that, but there was punishment. There was always punishment. If a guy went on charges, they didn't go on that much, but if a guy went on charges, it was a serious thing. He got punished. Within a month or so there would be a notice, "So and so suspended for a week." Now, guys go on charges and everything is held in abeyance. Guys go on charges ten times. I had one guy, he must have been on six, eight times and there were no decisions. He just kept on working and doing the same thing. But, there was much stricter, semi-military protocol than there is today.

When I came on a high school diploma was required. I don't think they had the GED, the equivalency. I don't think they had that in my time. A lot of them today are a hell of a lot more educated. A lot of them have college degrees, but a lot aren't as educated. Maybe they have a high school diploma, but they're not as educated as we were because when we got a high school diploma, you earned it. Today, I think, they go through high school, but high school doesn't go through them. They're passed on. So, in that respect, some of them aren't as well educated as we were, some of them are.

Overall, probably the ones who don't have the education drag the educational level of the department down. I don't know if the statistics would show that or not, or if you could even do any statistical thing like that, but in my opinion the fact that you're taking in people who don't really have the high school education that most of us had back in my day, I think that's downgraded the department. I've seen reports, I can't believe the spelling, not so much the punctuation; not too many people are great on punctuation, but the spelling and the punctuation where the sentences run together without a period. You know everybody basically knows the sentence and where to put a period. Some of these reports I've seen go on and on and on, no period. Commas, all right, a guy can miss a comma; a guy could miss an exclamation point, but a period?

F. Grehl: We were the young kids, all out of the service. A little bit wild. Being confined to strict discipline for all those times, now you get on the job. We found out the discipline was still a little strict, but the old timers didn't like us too much. Because we had an attitude, we kids had an attitude. The world owed us a living. We saved the world for you old guys and you wouldn't have this day without us. Those were the arguments going back and forth, most of them good natured. You wouldn't have this job. The Japanese would be here sitting in your seat if we didn't win the war. That's what would go back and forth. Many of them used to just hate the guts of these young kids who thought the world owed them a living for fighting the war.

There were a lot of old timers out there who loved the young kids coming in there because they liked to see the youth there. If you're reasonable, even at my age, I go down to the beach and I watch the kids have a good time playing volley ball and basketball because I enjoy someone having a good time. Things I can't do any more, at least somebody's doing it. The same was in the fire department.

The attitude toward officers was total respect and scared. The Deputy Chief was God. You didn't even talk to him unless you had permission almost to talk to him. It was like basically in the service. You were in the service and your lieutenants and captains and generals and all that were God. You didn't question anything that they said. Basically in the service it was emergency type things you were doing. You were told to do something and you did it in an emergency. The fire department was a lot like that except for the routine in and around the firehouse.

I'm still in contact with a lot of the chiefs throughout the state. Many of whom we studied with, younger fellows who we worked with. One of basic problems they're having in the fire departments today according to the New Jersey Fire Chiefs Association is discipline. Discipline problems come from a lack of respect for officers. They did a lot of research trying to find out what their problem is. Their problem is the people they're getting in the fire departments and police departments, they have the same problems by the way, is lack of discipline because the new generation never had any discipline. They never were in the service. When we went on the police or fire departments, we just got out of the service. We were subjected to two, three, four years of discipline. So when you went on the fire department it was just another thing, discipline. You learned to do what you were supposed to do.

Really what is discipline? Discipline is no more than the training of people to carry out their duties in an effective and efficient manner in accordance to the regulations you set in the department. That's all it is; discipline is people who do that. A lot of people think of discipline as being the negative type. We're going to fire you. There are seven steps of discipline. They holler at you, they reprimand, written reprimand and right down the line to the last one where they fire you. That's the other part.

There's a positive discipline which is again what I meant, training the people to do the correct things. Of course, when you can't train them, then you get into the other part which most of us understand as discipline. That's the negative part. So that's the basic difference when you said what was the fire department like? There was disciple there, lots of discipline. The things that we had to do everyday, you wouldn't believe. Every time we had a run with the apparatus, if it was raining when it came back everyone washed down the apparatus. Underneath, on top, dried it off, after every single run. You know today you're lucky you get it washed down once a week even if it's dirty. Lack of discipline I think.

Vesey: A lot of the newer kids didn't think like I did. Their thinking was entirely different. I don't say all, but the ones I came across. Some of them were all right. It's like the World War II guys and the Vietnam guys, the draft dodgers, the flag burners, and all that. It was the country that changed, so did some of the feelings in the fire department. I guess any job. Younger people have different ideas.

McCormack: There has been a tremendous change in the pension system. In those days, the whole society was different. Nobody retired before they were forty. I mean virtually nobody. I'm sure there were people who did it. Entrepreneurial types or types probably who made their billion dollars and quit when they were forty. It certainly wasn't the common thing. Don't forget for a lot of the guys, there wasn't even Social Security when they began. All they had was their pension. When I came on the job, in order to retire you had to meet two criteria. You had to be fifty-five years of age and had to have twenty-five years of service to retire. So, if you came on when you were twenty-one years of age, you would have your twenty-five years when you were forty-six years old. But you couldn't retire for nine more years, until you were fifty-five. By then you had thirty-four years on the job. That's the minimal time when you could retire.

Nobody retired at fifty-five anyway. They stayed until they were sixty-five. There was virtually nobody on this job who ever got out before being sixty-five. You simply stayed right through. You came on and stayed until you were sixty-five years of age. All they had was their pension and their pension was nothing. When I came on the job I was making twenty-four hundred dollars. The top pay was thirty-six hundred dollars. So, if you retired with half pay of thirty-six hundred dollars at sixty-five you would get eighteen hundred dollars. That was barely subsistence level. The working fireman was barely at subsistence level in those days. An old timer said to me when I came on the job, "Ain't a bad job kid. You'll wind up getting a house out of it and you'll get a pension, so you won't starve to death when you retire. But that's about all, you know." That's about it, as opposed to some blue-collar people who worked in factories. I guess because you had a steady job, you were able to get a mortgage on a building. You would live in it all your life and you would probably die in it. You would wind up owning a home in Newark and you'd have a pension when you retired. That's what your life would be. He was telling me you would never get rich on this job, but you won't starve to death. You'll wind up owning a home. That was the prospect for a fireman.

Freeman: The discipline I think is better now than it was, but I think it can be better. When I came on the job it was a little wild. In Twelve Engine, guys used to get drunk and break bottles, and tear up things. There was one long party every time they came to work. It may be that way now in some firehouses. But I don't think it's like it was and there wasn't that much discipline. Captains put up with it, but they didn't do anything about it. But I think now in the later years; that isn't put up with like it was. The professionalism has surfaced more than it was years ago. There's a little bit more professionalism. There was professionalism then. But I think the department has changed in training and professionalism. More professional than it was before.

I think we have better qualified personnel because of training. Years ago you studied which is good. Guys really studied and made chief; they knew what they were doing. Now you have training not only in your own department, but also in the national training areas and state training areas. You can go to training at the National Fire Academy. You can take courses. They have videos now that you can see in training. It's just better now than it was. Much, much more improved, but I would say you don't have the dedication that you had years ago. It's just a job to these guys. They don't have that dedication.

McGrory: The young guys coming on today, their educations probably are better than the educations of some of us who are on the job, but I don't know if they can apply it. Education can mean quite a different thing to different people. They may have four years of high school and four years of college, but they may not have the basic know how. Because we had guys who were jacks-of-all-trades you could draw upon. Plus there were a lot of intelligent fellows who may not had the degrees and the amount of years in school, but were intelligent people.

I don't know if the young guys' feelings for the job are the same or not. The feeling of everybody in the general population in this country has changed. The people don't have the same feelings towards their job, rightly or wrongly.

A lot of fellows who were in the field, they're lucky. You have to work and do your job. But a man says, "What you don't know won't hurt you." Well, what you don't know will hurt you, but you don't know it. I could see even in the field, what was happening; things that I couldn't believe. Little things like men calling chiefs by their first name. I thought it was time to leave. I saw a big change in the fire department. The fire department that I wanted to be in it was changing so much. I didn't really even understand. All this consent decree and it wasn't just that. I blocked a lot of it out. I just didn't want to know it. And also the things you couldn't get done. I mean for the better of everybody on the department, even when it came to the equipment, firehouses, and training. The city wasn't pulling together to get anything done. So, I figured I did have that time as the chief of the department. I did get that salary at that time, so it was probably a good time economically and for my own wellbeing to leave.

Denvir: As far as the firehouse is concerned, it's according to what your situation is and where you're located. Like here in Vailsburg, it's just like the old days, great bunch of guys. We have a lot of fun together. You eat your meals together. We play golf. I guess it's according to where you're located and the type of people you work with. It seems to be the same in most firehouses. Most of the guys get along. Firemen are easy to get along with. They usually pull together. I guess it's something to do with the job.

With this new testing we get a lot of good guys, but there are a lot slipping under the door that never would be on the job and it shows. From what I've seen, it can be dangerous.

Freda: When I first came on the job, one of the old timers told me going back in his time all the captains were German. Back when he was a young firefighter and it was totally military back then. They couldn't even lie in the bunkroom beds in the afternoon. If they wanted to take a nap, his captain would allow them. They had a little rug that they would lay in between the beds to sleep on. Nobody was allowed on the bed. Another thing that's changed is on multiple alarms the captain would hit the gong. Even though it was on the other side of Newark, we'd have to stay up while that multiple alarm was in existence. We knew we weren't going. Half the city would have to burn down, but that was the rule. We'd have to come down and stay downstairs while the multiple alarm was in progress.

Now people would think you're nuts if you would call the company down for a multiple alarm down neck. But you didn't know any better. You did these things and you accepted them. That's why you hear people say the job isn't like it used to be. The kids don't perceive it that way. They think this is the way it's always been. They fall into it and they like it. You're not going to impress them that the job is worse, or the job has changed. That's a fallacy in people's minds. When I first came on the job, the word semi-military certainly could be applied to the fire department. Right now I think it's just a loosely used term. There's no doubt in my mind that it has no meaning in the fire department today; except traditionally people still say semi-military organization. I think that's a falsehood because I don't think it's there anymore.

Miller: I think the educational level of some of the cadets who have come on the job now is much less than it was twenty, thirty years ago. At one time they were thinking of raising the standards to two years of college to get on the job. Or if you did get on the job, you would go to a program where you could get an associate degree and the city would help you along. Somewhere along the line, that was thrown out. That was really a good incentive for the personnel on the job and for people who want the job. If you really want something you'll try harder, you'll do a better job, and you deserve it because you put more into it. The exam is not the type of exam that we were given twenty years ago where it was a general IQ test or almost an SAT. Where you were asked a hundred and twenty five questions and you really had to know what you had to do. That doesn't affect the physical firefighting of the job. You can learn that part, but there may come a time in the future where there'll be a lot of Indians and nobody can be chief.

Carragher: Years ago you had tremendous experience on this job. You come on the job then, in two years you could know what you're doing, in two to three years, yes. Today you have guys with five years, what do they have five fires under their belt? Five years. I was in the Fourth Battalion for a little over nine years and when I left if you were four or five years on the job, you were a senior man in the Fourth Battalion. It went from senior men in the fire department being in the Fourth Battalion, to guys with a few years on the job who are senior men in the battalion. That shows you the transition. All the older men had to leave. It got too much. It did become a young fire department.

Now guys aren't exposed to it any more. The fire rate is probably going back to the pre-'60s. It's probably the same thing. We only had that fire down neck once every couple of months and Vailsburg only had it every couple of months and then Twenty-Nine Engine, Seventeen only had it once every couple of months and North Newark only had it every couple of months. That's where it is now. It's back to pre-'60s. It is exactly. When I first came on, you could tell the companies that went to fires and you could tell the companies that didn't go to fires. Then for a while, you started getting a lot of good companies. Not just the few that are in the central core. Now you started getting companies all over the city that were getting good. So, you only had very few companies that probably weren't peak. There were companies that weren't peak. But not like it was prior to the '60s. We're coming back now where I think we're going to have to get more into training, a lot more training. To teach these guys more. You can give them all the training you want in the Fire Academy or anyplace else. It's nothing when you get to a fire. You have to have the experience to do it. If you don't have it, you don't have it.

That's because of the retirements. I remember the time no one retired before they were sixty-five. Nobody left the job. It was unheard of. And then once in a while you heard a guy who left after twenty-five years on. One of my first captains in the Rescue Squad went out with twenty-five years. He was one of the very few who went out. He went out in probably 1966 or '68. Somewhere in that area he retired with twenty-five years on the job because he had an accounting degree and he wanted to be an accountant. Then you had to be fifty-five years of age also. But other than that, I don't recall too many people who can say they left with twenty-five years' service. It's only in the last ten, twelve years or fifteen years that guys started bailing out with twenty-five. Probably after the riots is when it started. But probably the biggest change to the attitude of, "Let me get the hell out of here with twenty-five" was the guys who came on in '59.

But you also have to remember that the period from '59 up until '80 was probably the biggest transition this fire department had ever seen as far as work. From slow to the busiest years, you went through the riots, all this turmoil in the city and everything. Guys burned out. They were burned out in the late '70s. The morale was there because of the spirit of work. Guys worked together good. The morale was tremendous and the guys loved the job. But like I was saying, they were being burned out. A lot of guys feel, "Hey, how long can I take this?" and guys started getting out. Maybe some of these guys if that have seen the fire department the way it is today. Maybe they would hang around.

On the other hand, the pension has become a lot more lucrative now too. The '20 Act I think was fifty percent, half pay and you had to be twenty-five years and fifty-five years of age. Now with the way the pension's changed today, you can get seventy percent at thirty years. You can see with the contracts; negotiations were long drawn out and you have to fight for everything.

When I came on the job most people were mechanical. They had a good mechanical ability because our entrance exam was a mechanical test. You had to have a mechanical aptitude to come on the job or you wouldn't make it. Today it's not mechanical. I don't know what the test is today, but we're not getting mechanical people. We're getting people on who don't know the first thing about their car, the first thing about their home, maybe because they have money. Years ago everybody was poor so everybody had to do for themselves, but today it's different. Or maybe it's even a technical society. They can't do it today. Whatever the reason, the guys are smart and you can teach them things, but they don't have the natural, normal background with them. People were naturals. There are no naturals today. I don't think.

Haran: It's a totally different job to me the last eight, nine years being up in the Burg than it was. But I'm just biding my time. I'm just putting time in. That's all I'm doing. Why a young kid would want to sit up there all the time and not try and get down into Six Engine or Eleven Engine or Eighteen Engine or Twelve Engine or Five Truck, Nine Truck, or Eleven Truck. Why they wouldn't want to do it is beyond me. How they can just come up there and sit. Obviously, they don't want to do anything. They don't want to do it. They just want a pay check, come in and rest from their part time work. That's the only thing I can see. Me? I wanted to go to fires and I still did my part time work. I don't know. I don't know.

Butler: It's now to a point where quite often most guys around the city have to be told to do housework. It used to be a standard thing. Nine o'clock the coffee cups away. Let's clean. I've got to remind these guys every once in a while, "Hey, nine thirty guys, it's house work time." Time to sweep or mop; whatever we have to do. We're fortunate here, almost all the floor surface that we really have to deal with, except the apparatus floor, is tiled. So, a quick broom and a damp mop keep it clean. But it's just that guys don't just get up and do it automatically anymore. Even at times you used to have one guy get up and get started, pick up the broom. Then everybody else would see it and decide, "Well yes, let's go." You don't have that guy anymore. You really have to say something to them.

As far as keeping the equipment clean, it's no where near like it used to be. It's just that I think of this house fairly fortunate that a few of the tours here they just feel they want to do it. Rather than being ordered or pushed to do it. We've made up our own little thing of who does what between a couple of the tours here. The stuff is kept reasonably clean and in decent order.

The quality of some of your officers, your first line officers and your chief officers, some of them might be great, great book men. They might be super guys and quote the page and the paragraph and the line that something they're stating came out of, but they don't have the ability to lead men at a fire scene.

The change didn't happen after the riots and the burnings of '68. Not right away, no. Guys still were proud they were firemen, had pride in the job; looked to do the best job they could. Later on, I'd say it got into the eighties, maybe around the mid-eighties, it seemed that right from the very top management of the department, seemed to start slacking off on the semi-military policies that they did have. Guys started getting sloppier in the firehouse. They weren't clean-shaven, dressed properly. And that started leading to a real deterioration where the only thing guys wanted to do is when the bell hit, go out and put a fire out.

They didn't care if the apparatus was clean or dirty. Didn't care if the axe heads were sharpened; didn't care for any of that stuff. Just leave me alone. I'll put the fire out. Training did drop off and your chief officer leadership seemed to be slacking. I think they went into a slack period because the top management wasn't really pushing for anything. They didn't feel that it was important to push the training aspect. When I first came on one of the two days a week you went out drilling. You had a multi-company drill. You were using water and ladders. You weren't just standing there talking about it.

Today, unless a couple of guys really want to get together and get the Battalion Chief, "Let's run a drill." it's virtually non-existent. That happened, I think, in the mid-'80's and just continued. Just a total lack of anybody really caring about training or teaching and just go out and put the fire out the best you can and so long, goodbye, and time to go back to the firehouse.

Aside from being down at the Academy for ethics and that hepatitis routine to see the movie and explanation of that, it's been well over two years since we've been to the Academy for any course. I think somebody is very remiss in that. It's got to start from the top. You can't tell me the people sitting up on Eighteenth Avenue don't know that there's no training going on down there. It's just that it's been just totally ignored and overlooked.

Wargo: You don't have the volume of fire anywhere in the city that you did maybe eight years ago, so it's going to reflect. The guys just don't pick up the experience. The experienced men are retiring. Morale, it isn't that it's bad; it's just that the guys are complaining mostly about the manpower. But I think that the expertise is lacking in a lot of the common evolutions. There seems to be a lack of training at the company level.

Prachar: Guys coming on the job now, you say do housework and they kind of like look at you. We're going out on a drill. "Why are we going out on a drill?" They question you. We're going to go to the Training Academy. Why are we going to the Training Academy? Everything is why. Myself, I still want to fight fires. Being in some companies that were on the outskirts, I just wanted to go in and get close to something. I would volunteer to move up. Why are we moving up? Years ago if you ever asked an officer why, you'd never ask that question again.

The attitude of some of the young guys is fire comes up, put out the fire. In the meantime I'm going to sleep. I'm going to watch television. I'm going to do this. But as an officer you go and say we're going to drill, why? Why? Because I want to, that's why. It's not like when I came on the job.

You're lucky you get some guys in at the time blow. We used to have joker circuits. At the time blows there was always a tick, tick from the joker and then the gong would hit. Well, there were guys we called tick, tick, boom. These were the guys who came in between the tick, tick and the gong ringing. Now you're lucky if you can get in touch with the guy sometimes a quarter after eight, eight-thirty. They may live only a short distance away. Say, "Hey you're late for work." "Oh, if I'm late for work, I'm late for work." I was never like that. When I was in Rescue, we were coming in at seven o'clock days. Even now they still do it, the crew that's up there. If you worked nights and an alarm came in at seven o'clock, you didn't even get out of the rack because you knew they were all downstairs. Certain houses you have to get out of the rack at five to eight to see if you have to go or somebody's in. It's just different, the attitudes of everybody. But yet the guy who comes in at one minute to eight is looking for the man at five o'clock to get out of there. He wants to be the first relief.

The disciplinary problem started when all the garbage started with the captain's test when they didn't make captains for X amount of years. You had companies with acting captain for five years, then they get a promotion and a captain goes into this spot. Well, now you're infringing on this guy's benefits because these guys have been running their own company. Now you come in there and say, "I'm the boss. This is the way it's going to be." I bet you when they started making all these big groups of captains, if you look at the transfer list it was a lot of these guys who didn't have officers for a long time who transferred out. Because they ran the company the way they wanted to as firefighters as well as they should have because they were the acting captain. But when the captain came in, if it wasn't being run their way, the guy just left and started anew with an officer someplace else.

Some of the people who are coming on because of the effects of the lawsuit don't want to do the job. They're just coming on because they could ride down the street with a fire truck with its red lights going, sirens, air horns, and wave to their friends. Then you have some guys who fight and work to get on this job. I worked the last two courses with the guys from Community Relations. Guys coming out to train for the job, you knew who wanted this job. There's a class in the Academy now, I bet you ninety-five percent of them went to that class every day because they wanted this job. Not have it handed to you. White or black, they were there. I could take you out there and show you every guy out there who was up there every night working their ass off. But these guys want the job, so you're getting a better class of guys who want it.

McDonnell: There's been a gradual erosion of interest in this department. The Fire Chief stopped going to fires, stopped the annual inspections. We used to have quarterly inspections. All of that stuff just gradually died. You started seeing the lack of discipline, people not doing what they were supposed to and nothing happening to them. All the ranks, it just drifted down. They lost their morale.

Then we had the wonderful affirmative action which gave us less qualified people coming on the job, less capable. In my time on the job, that was the biggest change I saw. The difference I noticed after '81; I was a captain, I saw this. If you asked me if there is any difference between the guys who came on later in my career as opposed to in the beginning, I'd say that there was less intelligence, definite, definite. It's not everywhere, not every guy but, in general that's how I saw it.

I was a school teacher and I noticed that. There was a big difference in when I would sit guys down and go over a drill or a lesson. Talk about how we do this. You could see. In five minutes their heads would be wondering around. They had no attention span. They couldn't transfer knowledge. If you tell them something, they couldn't take that one thing to something else, to another situation and apply it. You'd tell them the same thing over and over again. Go in one ear and out the other. They are different than the people who were there before. That was the big change that I noticed.

We got a lot more people with problems. Not that you didn't have them before. Whatever you had before in the way of negative things, you got more of them and less of the good. You still get excellent people. You used to have problem people before, but you got more of them. The percentage of them increased. The biggest thing was you don't have to study for promotional exams anymore. Even the guys who worked for me; they said the exam's a joke. Anybody, any idiot can pass. Who knows what the passing grade was. They could make it five.

We had a loss of leadership at the top and we lost competence at the bottom. Together they just really put a hurting on this department. I saw that over the years at fires. The younger guys don't know any better. They don't know. This is the way it is. How could they know? If you were around longer, you could see what was done then as opposed to what's done now. Or what was done when I left the job. But it did go downhill. It's not something I'm glad to say. I always wondered if it's our fault. I mean the guys my age, my era, because we came into the department when it was great. Maybe we should have fought. We should have said something. We should have stood up. Or we should have not let it happen.

I think because of the loss of morale, maybe they didn't do it. Years ago, if a guy was a problem, he didn't say anything. If he stood up and said, "We should do this." He'd get beaten up. The older guys, the guys who were on before me wouldn't tolerate that. You were going to do your job or that was it. You were going to be a fireman or get the hell out of here. You think the department is still a great job. It was a good job when I came on. It was a good job when I left. I just think that, unfortunately, the department declined.

The types of people are different. I don't see as many people who have an interest in it. I don't know if it's a loss of the work ethic or whatever. I don't know if it's just general to society, to the country, but you just don't seem to get people who care as much; people who it means something to them personally to do a good job. Most people when I came on the job that I met or I worked with seemed to care about doing a good job, much more than when I left the job. The older guys, we were kind of disgusted. You talk to the young guys, they love the job. Maybe it's just getting old. When you were new, this was great. You talk to them, it's great. It's terrific. The job itself is pretty much the same. The department has changed dramatically, but the job, no.

Pianka: When I came on, most of the firemen were old timers. The real old timers were off in the Burg. When I went up there on a detail or on overtime, I was shocked. First of all, they all had gray hair and big pot bellies. You say, "Where did these guys come from?" But they were from the old school. They were hanging around until they were hitting sixty-five because that's what you did. You worked until you were sixty-five. It was after that period that there was a dramatic change. For a guy who came on in the early '70s, you saw all these men who hung around until they're sixty-five.

Then all of the sudden things shifted. They changed the retirement requirements. You no longer had to have twenty-five and be at least fifty-five. You could go after twenty-five years and guys just started to bail out. So, a guy like me with thirty years on the job is very rare. There are very few people left who were around when I came on. All you have to do is look at the seniority list. I'm one of the senior men, with thirty years. I bet if you go back to the '60s, there were a lot more guys doing forty years at least. That's a big change. There was a period in the '70s and '80s that we were fairly busy. I guess you did your twenty-five. Hey, I'm out of here.

We had window days and brass. The early '70s is the tail end of that really going on. I went to Six Engine with Deputy Chief Donlon and he required it. It was even more important doing it in a chief's house. We did the brass on certain days, windows on certain days. You weren't as pressured in Five Truck as you were in Six Engine because Six is a chief's house. That slowly went by the wayside with the brass. A lot of things nowadays aren't done like they used to be done. If there was a second alarm sounded whether you went or not everybody was supposed to hit the floor and that's what we did. Of course after a half hour, you went back upstairs. Now if they could they would just turn over in bed, but a second alarm, you're going because there are fewer companies, especially a company like Seven Engine.

Another thing these guys used to do. They smoked a lot more. That's the big difference too. Back then, I don't remember guys working out. Nobody was health conscious. Everybody smoked. Nowadays, go upstairs, there's a weight room right here on the second floor. Every firehouse has weights. Guys work out. They don't drink as much in the firehouses. Guys smoke a lot less. They're healthier. Back then they weren't. No wonder we had that one year with so many of those guys dying. It took its toll on them, sad to say. It probably still does to some degree.

The department is much younger. Almost every one of those thousand guys who were on the job when I came on has retired. They left the fire department much younger. There was a transitional period again, going back to that racial thing. That started to bother a lot of guys because tests were changed. People got left on lists, various things, which sort of got in the way of good morale. People bounced back from that more or less. It wasn't the end of the world, let's put it that way. I'm not going to make a judgment of whether it was good or bad. It was the law of the land and sometimes maybe things work out better than you realize they worked out.

I think this fire department is in just as decent shape as it ever was. Let's face it, there are people still out there working. They have the same attitude I had when I came on. A lot of young kids come on, want to be on this job, enjoy it. Like the tradition, want to put fires out. I don't see much difference in that respect, other than superficial stuff. Apparatus is different. Turn out gear is different. Some of the fires are going to be different.

That's the thing that I foresee that's going to be the big difference. The fires are going to be different. Because construction is different, materials being used are different. In a way it's going to get worse for these kids.

Because I remember going into three story frames that should have never stood. When we finally put the fire out, you looked around. You'd say, "There's nothing left." They're still standing. I can't see that happening with these new buildings. So, I don't know. I worry for them, the future generations.

I can associate with every one of these kids who walks in. I know how they feel. It doesn't seem that long ago. It's thirty years ago, but I can still remember how I felt when I came in. I know a lot of these guys want to do a good job. All they need is somebody to say, "Hey kid, just hang onto me or hey the fire's over here. Don't be afraid, we're with you." That's all they need, most of them. And most of them are willing. A lot of these young kids, I give them a lot of credit. They're just as good as anybody else who was around thirty, forty, fifty years ago. I can honestly say that. I don't feel the job has degraded because of the new people in any way. I really don't. I have a lot of respect for these kids and I think they do a good job.

I don't think there's been any change in why people take this job. Ultimately you need a job and you stumble into this thing and you make of it what you want. It could either be drudgery or it could be a happy time, a good time. I think if it worked thirty years ago, the same thing applies. This job right now today probably in many ways is more dangerous than it was thirty years ago when I came on, even though we have better equipment. You're still getting beat up.

Rotonda: Now we're getting a change of attitude. In the type of people coming on the job, but also in the people who make the job function properly, it's going to the dogs. See, Uncle Joe always said that it takes longer to build quality, but it out lasts quantity in the long run. We're not getting quality anymore. We're not getting quantity either, but we're not getting quality, definitely.

Ryan: Probably the biggest change that came on the fire department was the way the captain was in charge of the firehouse and he really controlled it. Without a captain there, things can tend to be more lax and not get done. It's the old, "You can't tell me to do that. Oh, we'll do it tomorrow." There was a period of approximately eight years where there were no captains promoted and that was a serious problem. It was a serious problem in the firehouses for the newly promoted captains after that to come back and wrest control from a group of people who they had probably worked with and yet weren't used to doing this regular routine.

There was no continuity of leadership and basically companies were left on their own. You need someone in charge, not just somebody acting in charge. You honestly need someone there to oversee what's going on in that company. Not only in the field, at fire operations or drills, but in the firehouse to make sure that all the necessary things get done. Whether it's training evolutions or normal maintenance, cleaning, without somebody there to tell them to do it, it's difficult to motivate people to do it. The Battalion Chief honestly can't be on top of all his companies. He can't be the captain of the firehouse. That's why you need a captain there to be in charge of and maintain everything that's going on. That was a real problem.

The discipline is a lot less rigid, in the firehouse especially. I lay it back to those years when we didn't have a captain's list. And that was something very hard to recover from. When I came on there were a lot of people who had been in the military or whose family had been in the military and they were used to doing things very rigidly. It's just a societal change. You don't have that now. We still get a smattering of veterans coming in.

They're easier to handle because they know the discipline. "No, you can't do that." "Oh, okay. You can't do that." Some of the younger people don't have that self-discipline.

Carter: There have been severe changes in the way fires are fought since I've been on the job. It used to be like a cavalry charge to see who could get the first water on the fire. I mean literally, maybe fist fights, early on in my career. Twenty Engine would try to run up the back of Six Engine. People would fight to go to more fires, more runs. One day Kenny Marcell and I got in a fight in a liquor store on Broadway and Sixth Avenue. They're trying to cop Fifteen's line. We had moved it in and we were hitting the fire. They said, "Hey, take a blow. We got it." "Get your own line. You guys are slugs from Four Engine. Give me a break." That started to change and I would be hard pressed to say when, other than sensing of swing throughout the '80s. We've arrived at the '90s where the firefighting capability of the department is very spotty. The veterans are gone. The people from the '59 list who were the old pros when I came on are almost all gone. And the guys who saw the riots, just a handful left. The people who knew firefighting. There wasn't a complete and total transfer of knowledge because we've started to slow down. Guys would retire and the knowledge wouldn't pass. So now we have a generation that's split.

Still some dynamite people out there who learned it in the '70s and '80s, but a lot of people from the latter part of the '80s just don't know what the hell they're doing. And now there's a newer generation evolving that doesn't want to know anything except watching cable TV. They don't even know how to fight fires. There are people who specialize in holding doors for the busy companies who can go in and put out the fire. Make it easier for them. So there has been a great diminution of the skill level of the Newark Fire Department in my seventeen and a half years.

I would say more people take the job for security now, but there are still those who want to be fire lads. When I took the job, on the state-wide advertisement you had people who desperately wanted to get in and start kicking some serious fire ass in the big city. Guys like Pete Partridge. Guys like Joey Ryan. And myself, I was a volunteer before I came on the job, then I was in the Air Force and Rahway and I wanted to go to fires. We got guys now who want a pay check and more than I care to think about, seriously.

Langenbach: When I made captain, firefighters still had respect for officers. But you could see it starting to go with the new kids coming on the job. You could see it staring to go when they start calling you "cappy" instead of captain. Yes, you could see it starting to go and I always hoped I wasn't like a dinosaur that I wasn't holding onto things that were in the past, but I never understood the mentality of the new kids coming on. Today, even more today, I definitely don't understand it. We saw that shift away from the veterans, predominantly veterans coming on the job, to now we're getting a non-veteran. There was a little loss of respect. I never felt I was being disrespected, but some of these guys would push it to the limit.

Some of the old school of going out and drilling all the time that slowly disappeared, too. McGrory was an old school chief. He would go out and drill. Some places wouldn't do that. Well, you're learning it out in the field. Yes, you are, but as the field work slowed down, the drills never picked up again. Headquarters, in their ultimate wisdom, just assumed everything was okay. You'd pass out the drill schedules every quarter and you assume that everybody's doing it. I don't know the last time anybody's drilled other than you drill with a new rig or you realize you have a problem. You go drill with a ladder raise or we have a new mask, let's drill with that. We drilled a lot with haz-mat when I was assigned to the Academy, but not a lot of actually drilling for firefighting. We didn't do as much as we should have, that's for sure. In Six we didn't do as much as I guess they had done maybe in the '50s. Again the theory was you're going to learn it out on the street, so you don't need to drill. Sure there was a time frame that probably held true.

Luxton: The attitude of firefighters to officers has probably changed since I came on. I think the officers are more approachable than they were. The officers used to be stricter. For instance the phone might ring four times today. Now that wouldn't happen before. The house watch would pick up by two rings. You can't get that through anybody's head, but at the same time I can't fault them. The phone did get answered and I didn't tell them to wash the truck and that thing is shiny right now. I don't know. Am I wrong in not enforcing that phone thing. Who knows? There's part of the problem, probably, people like myself being more lax in what used to be protocol in the '50s and '60s.

Is that the fault of my generation of officers or has the department itself become lax in enforcing that? The officers are the department. If you didn't answer the phone in the '60s, you might have gone on charges. Now, they've done away with that. It would be a shame to ruin some guy's career because he didn't answer the phone. There were probably a lot of times when things like that happened, but there were also times when people drove the fire engine and they had been drinking, which was also wrong. I don't know. I really don't know. But the deterioration of the fire department definitely has to do with officers like myself. We're in tune and maybe we just didn't make the guys who work for us as in tune as we are. I'm no different than some of these other guys. I don't think my training was any different.

Connell: The biggest difference is the people we're getting on the job now. When I came on, the country had gone through a period of wars over the years. The Second World War, the Korean conflict, the Vietnam War, so it was over a long period of time where there weren't men who had not served time in the service coming on the job. So, we were more willing to accept what had to be done when it was told to us to do it without asking questions. Today the biggest change in the people coming on the job is we're not as busy now as we were then. We're getting fewer fires, but the guys who don't know the difference think they still are the busiest and the best that ever walked the earth. They don't have the discipline because there are very few if any who came on the job in the last ten years that are veterans. A lot of them don't have the work ethics of veterans or people who grew up in the '50s and the '60s. They are a bunch of great guys. They're eager beavers, but to me they seem very immature.

But I wonder what the veteran firefighters thought about us when we came on. I can only tell you what I think. I thought we were pretty good and my understanding was most people did. I'm sure some veterans said the same thing that I'm saying today. It's just that our group was more involved. When there was a racket, we all went to the rackets. We hung out together. We partied together. We worked together. We were a close family. Today's "x" generation, they seem to be, "What's in it for me?" They're the "me" generation instead of the "we" generation.

There isn't any discipline or morale anymore. We got a notice from the Director six months ago about discipline and how they're going to start strictly enforcing it. Nothing has changed since his directive came out. Morale is waning. There's no direction. The fire department seems to be floundering now since the Fire Chief and the Director no longer talk to each other. Nothing is really getting done and when training comes I have the Director calling me up, telling me to go one way with training and I have the Fire Chief calling me up, telling me to go in a completely different direction. So, I usually do middle ground and try to please them both without telling either I changed their directives.

Perdon: The job changed big time since I came on. It's going to keep on changing and not for the better. It's just a sign of the times. You've gotten slower. The newer guys coming on just have a different mentality. That's not putting them at fault or anything, but it shows up in their work ethic. What they think they do at a job and what the job is to you or me, it's like they're so far removed from it. And in all due respect though too, you have to give the guys who do the job well and are brand new, as slow as we are, if they can go in and do a good job, you have to tip your hat to them just because of the lack of work. That's one of those things where, as busy as we were, it was demanding because you were so busy, but that's what made doing the job so easy. It made it just another day, another fire.

Now here these kids have to work a fire, a good fire, far and few between. If you could find that rare kid out there who shows up and does a good job with such a small amount of work, you have to tip your hat to the kid. I'm looking for him. I need a couple here.

Bisogna: There are younger guys who want to change things and the older guys who say this is the rule, the way it's always been and the way it should be right or wrong. A lot of times they're wrong, but that's the rule and they try to stick with it. Change in this job is a hard thing to take. Like I said, we were crying about them closing Prince Street and Shelly said, "Oh, take it easy, everybody is here with their face in their hands moaning how they're closing our firehouse. It's the way it is." After the change happens, "Oh it wasn't so bad." As you get older, change is harder to deal with. So, people like the status quo.

Well as soon as somebody says we're going to change something, guys throw their hands up and they're all upset about stuff, which it shouldn't be. I mean change is not a bad thing. These gradual changes have made it a better fire department than it was say ten years ago. I think more guys get along now because sure there are more minorities who you're working with and you realize, "Hey, they're just like you and I." But when you don't know something, you're afraid of it. So, that's part of the reason too. They didn't take my job. They may have taken some other Caucasian's job, but that's not my problem either. Whoever's got the job, as long as he's doing it; that's okay.

The only drawback to it is the relaxing of the standards. They did some relaxing, so you get officers who may not be as qualified as they were in the past, book knowledge or whatever. So the Training Academy has to say, "Okay we have to make sure everybody's at least knowledgeable in SOPs, in tactics and stuff like that." Even if a guy can't read in a book and learn it or get help from his friends studying together, at least there's somebody he can go to, some minimal training so we're all on at least the same starting page. That was a concern.

Now you get chiefs who came up through the ranks, but they may not have the same knowledge of a chief twenty years ago. They had to be pretty book smart back then. He had to be able to read a book and understand it and know tactics. But then you had idiots out in the field anyway then, too, who didn't have a clue. Could recite it front wards and backwards, but when it came to putting it into practice they might have been nervous. You get a real nervous idiot. He's great at test taking, but he's at a fire scene, not the right guy to be there. But he's your boss. This is a good job even for chiefs because they could just stand back and watch, most of the time the fire goes out anyway. A chief will make a good call, but even if he makes no call except to throw people at it, eventually the stuff goes out. They're all out now, right?

Has there been a generational change on the job? I heard that when I got on. I heard it last week. I think it's the same complaint. It's like you talk about your kids the way your father talked about you. It's the same. I mean for better or for worse things change. I remember looking at Eddie Camuso sleeping on the couch with a newspaper over him. Thinking, "Look at the new breed." I'm on the job ten years, thinking, "Look at this idiot, he's on the job a year." Not that ten years is an old salt, but still you're looking down. "What are we hiring bums now?" But who knows what they said about me when I might have fallen asleep at the kitchen table. I don't know. Look at this guy sleeping on the bench. I think that's just the way life is. I don't think it's generations. You can point to any specific generation and say, "Look what they did, ruined everything." I think it's just a gradual change for better, for worse just like it is in your life with your children or anybody's generational change. Like I said, the older people don't like change.

Ricca: When I came on George Caswell was senior man at Nine Truck. Myself, Tony Peters, and Bobby Langevin had between the three of us just the academy under our belts. Langevin was the next in line to senior man and he was on the job I think eight months at the time. Now the new kids have to go down neck because there's no room on the hill.

We could go down neck on our tour and I see kids that I have no idea they're fireman. And you ask somebody in the crew, "Who's that?" And they shrug their shoulders, "I don't know." Everything up on the hill is filled. It's steady. I've been with the same group of guys now eight years.

There have been changes in the way we fought fires it seems. Change in the people coming on. Not everywhere, not the Fourth Battalion, being bias, the Fourth Battalion though we always did things differently. Just for some reason it always did. Just the guys coming on and we're starting to lose the camaraderie of your company. Not all companies, we stayed pretty close, even though like our group lived in different places, but the going out and hanging out. The meeting at a place before you came in. A lot of that stuff just went out the window. Guys complaining that the job sucked while they had their feet up drinking a beer and having a sandwich; watching the sports game with the air conditioner on. It started to change with some of the old guys too. And I think it was we started having less and less fires. We always noticed that. We'd start getting on each others nerves. Tommy would be the first one to say, "We need a fire." But it just seemed like the new guys coming on, you'd start helping them, teaching them about the job and it would be, "When do we get paid? When's uniform allowance? Do I have to wear a shirt?" Stuff like that, that was the ground work of the demise of the department.

I'd say the whole '70s were great. If you want to use the '80s as a decade in whole, that would be a good time to say these changes started. You started losing guys who knew Newark at its good hay day and it's greatness. They just treated the job differently. When I came on the job, I lived in Newark. I had a lot of pride in not only that I was a fireman, but I was a Newark fireman. To this day, somebody asks me, I'm not a fireman, I'm a Newark fireman. But you lost that and it's really getting worse and worse and worse. I'm fortunate right now, I went to Twelve Engine when I got promoted and I had a good bunch of guys and I still have a good bunch of guys, guys that care. You could tell when you go out on a first aid call if the guy has compassion or at a fire, if you don't leave the nozzle open and throw it on the floor. You leave the nozzle open and hang it out the window or you undo the butts when you're in the hall way rather than in somebody's apartment. I think we're just losing that.

The change in the physical and the written in the test brought on the advent of not lowing standards for one particular group, but for all groups. So you don't get the all-around guy that you got. Another bad thing I think is the eighteen year old age. You get a kid that never worked a day in his life, comes to this job and doesn't appreciate it. But get somebody that dug ditches for a few years or did some labor, now they get this job. Now they appreciate, where when you work you work hard, but when you play you play hard. I think that's where we're losing. And these young kids, it's just a pay check and three days off. A few of the new kids from the last class came by. Out of three guys, two were extremely interested in what I was talking about. The other guy could care less. After everything was over it's like, "Could I go to lunch now?" or "What are we having for lunch?"

I try to impart to the guys. You don't remember, we had to book every run and book return taps. I teach the guys all that. As a matter of fact, whenever somebody new comes up, I make him do the book like we did in the old days, only so they get a piece of tradition, a piece of knowing what it was like. I think all of that is what brought us the pride, from the booking of the runs to the cleaning of the apparatus. You're supposed to wash the truck.

You don't bitch and moan. We have to wash the truck. It's dirty. You're here for ten hours, make the most of it.

I think we're losing it and we're losing it because we don't have fires. Fires are too few and far between. You messed up at a fire before, fifteen minutes later, a half hour later, the bell was going off and you were going to get your second crack at what you screwed up on. The first time I ever had a line in my hand, I get Eighteen's line. Jackie Denvir was the captain. We start pushing in and I'm a truck man. I wouldn't let go of my tool. As I'm going in and I open the door to where the fire was, but when I opened the door they would lighten up. I hit my head against the door and shut it. I opened the door again. Everybody started lightening up. I hit my head against the door and shut it. It happened three times. Finally, I handed the line to whoever was in back of me. I think it was Ray Frost as a matter of fact, and I walked out. I said, "I screwed up." Half hour later the bell came in and we had a fire. I made sure I grabbed a line, ventilated, and did what I had to do because I had to redeem myself. Now if you screw up in May, you may not be able to redeem yourself until December.

The day of the interior attack is probably going to be gone in ten years. It's going to be definitely gone with the turn over of people and the experience and knowledge not being passed down. Not having the book knowledge or the experience of six, seven, or eight fires in a tour. There are guys on the job from the last class who probably haven't seen a good working fire. So they don't know how to handle it.

Gesualdo: Initiative, incentive, the aggressiveness, the wanting to do something as opposed to just standing by and being told to do something. I don't see the same enthusiasm in the younger firefighters. I don't know whether it's because of the increase in the wages, whether it's the friction between the different cultures and ethnic groups, but I don't seem it get the same sense of importance to the job. Being on time doesn't seem to be a real big issue anymore, the hour early. There was friction in the past, "Oh, to hell with you. You're not coming in at five o'clock; I'm not coming in at seven o'clock." And I think those little things have all probably culminated in this new mentality, which is "Whatever is good for me."

When we first came on, it was like whatever is the best for everybody. How's the situation going to be better for everybody? Now it seems to be more whatever is going to benefit me. Guys walk in the door now, not on my tour but on other tours, I won't allow it, but they'll walk in the door and won't even check in with you, let you know they're here. They'll come in. They'll go upstairs. Some will be out all night or working a night job. Come in, go to bed. You don't even know whether they're there or not. That would have never happened twenty years ago. You didn't come in and not tell your captain you were here. Because I remember working as a bartender, rolling in here sometime at four o'clock in the morning, but I always remember setting the alarm so at seven o'clock, seven thirty I was up and told my captain I was here. It's just that kind of initiative to be responsible. I guess that's the best word. The newer generation doesn't seem to be as responsible. They seem to be a little more laid back and whatever is good for me.

Chapter Seven: Recommending the Job

Fredette: I loved the job; hated to get out; and I'd recommend it.

Kinnear: I enjoyed the job. Looking back, I was going to college and often think if I had not taken the job, where would I be? I was studying accounting and if I had completed college, I would probably be working in an office somewhere or would have worked in an office, with a briefcase and commuting. I watch my neighbors commuting to New York and I don't envy them. It's at least an hour commute in the morning, an hour commute back. I see them coming home six and seven o'clock at night. Dragged out. Tired. Looking at it that way, it was a good choice.

I would have been on the ground floor of a lot of things, too. Right after the war, I would have been one of the first ones out of college. There would have been a million opportunities. I often think of that, but really I have no regrets because I mostly enjoyed the job. I mostly liked the job. The camaraderie we talked about and all that. I still have friends. I wouldn't change. I wouldn't change it, no. I just wish the attitude on the job had stayed. The motivation, which is somewhat less now with some people, the camaraderie, the friendships, and everything had stayed. But that has to do with growing up, I guess. Over the ages everything changes and, like I said, it's looking at it from an older man's viewpoint. "These kids today, they don't know anything. You're not to do this." A lot of it's that I'm sure.

But I would recommend the Newark Fire Department to certain people. It's still a great job. For a guy with just a high school education or equivalency, where can you go and get that kind of money? Where can you go and get those kinds of benefits? Where could you go and get the friendships? This isn't an accurate way to put it because it sounds like I'm running the fire department down when I say it this way, yes, I'd recommend it to a guy who didn't have any aspirations to college or didn't have an idea of a career goal; didn't know what he wanted to do with his life. That sounds bad that way. I don't mean it that way because certainly firemen are as dedicated or as smart as people who go into the professions. I would recommend it to certain people, yes.

Redden: Oh, I enjoyed it tremendously. I made a lot of good friends. I have friends to this day that I made on the fire department. I enjoyed the camaraderie. Down at Sixteen Engine we used to go to Broadway shows together. We had firehouse picnics. Of course, that started to go away as people moved out of town and people worked part-time jobs. They just didn't have the time anymore for that type of thing, but you still had the good feeling for each other. I refer to the fire service as the last brotherhood, really. It is. It is. Because you can go into any firehouse and identify yourself, that you've been in the fire service or you're in the fire service and the doors open up.

That being said, I wouldn't recommend the job. I think a young man could do a lot more with himself today than going on the fire department. I really do. It's a different situation entirely. There are many smaller departments in Jersey now where they don't have a fire chief. If you're not a class A city you can appoint. It can be a political appointee, which is basically not a fire chief. No, I wouldn't recommend it.

Masters: I'd recommend it to anybody, absolutely. It's all according to the education they have. I enjoyed my job, but if they go to high school which they will do and maybe to college. It's all according to the education. If he's got the brains to make a good living, go. If he likes the fire department, what can you do? You still can go up the ranks of the fire department if you study. When I went on the job, the pay difference between a Captain and a fireman was about three hundred dollars. I got to do all this studying to get three hundred dollars? And then if you get a drunk you've got problems? No, I enjoyed being a fireman. I enjoyed the job and looked forward to going to work, helping people. In fact today I still help people. You don't forget.

F. Grehl: I enjoyed the job very much, very much. I was into that comradeship in the army where you're sitting in a fox hole and you're depending on the guy next to you. He's depending on you. You formed a comradeship. We had basically the same thing except instead of two guys we had four or five. They were good days really. It was like going to the club house. With the Blue Brothers, you laughed all the time. I told you Teddy Smith and Bernie Havic and all the rest of them. They were good times. You laughed and had a good time. I always used to say, when I'd be writing reports dealing with troubles in the firehouses, "Boy, if all I had to do was put out fires this would be the easiest job in the world." What you had in the firehouse, the majority of them, was like a club house. You go to the club house. You have a good time. That bell strikes. Everybody forgets everything else and out the door they go and they do their job. Then they come back, "Now where were we?" And they start all over again. But it was good, good comradeship, good team work. It was team work.

But I enjoyed the days. I'd do it again. Of course, I thought the same as my father when my son went to go on the fire department that he'd be better off, could make more money elsewhere. He had a college degree. He should have used it. I think he was a lot like me. He liked the outdoors, comradeship. I think he's content and happy where he is.

Vesey: I did enjoy the job. I wouldn't give it a hundred percent, but I'd say yes. I enjoyed a lot of it. I say, even ninety percent of the job. There's the pay. I tell you, I regret I never made the gray.* I never studied. I didn't have the temperament to apply myself. I'm not moaning about it. You get what you put into it.

I would recommend it. If they don't like it they could always quit. The hours, the pay is a lot better. There are a lot of jobs out there that aren't paying that much. As long as a guy doesn't mind working an occasional weekend or nights, that's the only drawback I can see.

McCormack: I still enjoy the job. I have no regrets. As far as recommending the job, let me put it to you this way. I always advocated education in the sense that, I felt if you got an education you open up all kinds of possibilities; of interesting possibilities of what you might do. You see, I didn't go to college. Like I say, I always thought that if you went to college and got a college education, a specialization in something or other, it would open up all kinds of possibilities, broaden your perspective of things you might do. But yet even with that said I realize a lot of guys get good educations and come right back and become firemen. So would I recommend it? Yes, I'd recommend it to my son in the sense that, if you like the job, there isn't a better job in the world. You know, in the spectrum of jobs, I think it's a great job. All things considered, I think this is a great job. Yes, I would recommend it to my son, but I would never force him on it or say you're going to be a fireman. It's the only thing you can be. Don't try anything else. My attitude was, if he wanted to be a farmer, a forest manager, a deep sea diver, or if he wanted to be a junk man and go around picking up scrap metal, whatever he wanted to do was okay with me. It's his

---

* At the time, captains wore gray uniform shirts.

life. He's got to do what he wants to do. He can't do what I want to do because I like it. He might hate it. It turns out he likes it.

Masterson: I enjoyed the job a lot. Oh, yeah, I liked the job. You got to like the job to stay on with no money. Now that the pay is worthwhile, I'd recommend it. I wouldn't recommend it in risk. Not the way city hall is down there now. No, I don't think I could handle that. I would recommend the job to somebody who would go out in some of these smaller towns or something like that where they're paying good money. The work, I'd recommend the work. If they wanted to go to Newark, fine. New York? New York is good, looks good too. But Newark, I think it's gone downhill from the things different people tell me. Nobody ever tells me anything good, but we always complained too. I don't know the whole thing is, in my mind, about city hall, that administration down there, firemen, they're second class citizens. The only reason the money is there is because they have so many black firemen that there now. That's why they're getting all the benefits of all the work that was done before them. I hope they appreciate it because it's great benefits today the way I understand. But I don't think I would work in the city. I liked it better with the three story frames. Now they're all gone.

Deutch: Yes, I did enjoy the job. My lungs probably didn't, but I did. I probably wouldn't recommend it for my son if he was looking for a job. I probably wouldn't recommend it in the big cities. In a town like Belleviile maybe, Bloomfield, or Clifton I'd probably recommend it. But I would worry about him in Newark. Although I get the impression that a lot of firemen's sons are going on the job today and they love it because it's a good job for them. It's a job that's there. They're not worried about them. But I think I would be.

Wall: Yes, I enjoyed the job. I enjoyed being a firefighter. I wouldn't recommend it. If somebody said to me, "Is your son going to be a fireman?" I'd say, "I'd break both his legs if I thought he was going to be a fireman." I always considered it be a job, a dirty, hardworking job. When I was with the fire administration, I was the highest civil servant in the fire administration. My boss, the fire administrator was a Presidential appointee. The early ones were good men. Clyde Braggan, who I still correspond with, was the retired fire chief of Los Angeles County. They have a bigger fire department than half the standing armies of the world. I think he had six sons; two of them are firefighters. He said, "You'd never encourage your son to be a fireman?" I said, "No." And then we started talking about the difference in the job. A firefighter on the West Coast is a different job than a firefighter on the East Coast.

First off, they don't have that stuff called ice and snow which makes the job a lot different. And most of them, unless you're in south central LA, you're dealing with one family houses that have nice separations. And most of the work is that of a medical technician. A lot different job than we have here. As a result, their traditions are different than ours. I've experienced a lot of those departments when I was in the fire administration. And I was always impressed. The West Coast seems to have a much higher level of discipline than we experience on the East Coast. Don't forget, I'm an old union man. So, I'm not knocking the union. Except for San Francisco, there's very little tradition in labor unions in the fire service. Even though they are IAFF, they're not militantly IAFF. New York has always been a strong union town and we've accepted that tradition over here.

Freeman: I love the job even after thirty-five years. Citizens look up to you as a firefighter. How many adjectives can I use to explain that? I like to help. I guess it's the dangerous aspect of it. It's an uplifting type job for my personality. So, it's good. I like the job. That's why I'm still here after thirty-five years.

I'd recommend it to my son. If you don't have anything to do; if you don't have another goal in life; and you're looking for a good job, well, then hey, this is a good job because you can always do something else while you're on the job. Then I would explain a lot of other things, the danger, the long term, the short term risks. Yes, I would want my son to be a firefighter. I would recommend it, if he wanted the job. That would be his decision, not mine. But I would explain the job to him and say, "Look, if you don't have anything else to do, give it a shot. You can always quit the job if you don't like it and do something else." But I think once he came on the job and experienced the benefits with the time off and what else you can do on the job, then I think anybody would like it. But you have to have a certain dedication. You just can't take the job and feel that it's like an everyday job, like going out in the factory working forty hours a week. And I don't want to go to work today and you don't go. Sure I would recommend it.

McGee: Did I enjoy the job? I loved it. Would you recommend it today? Yes. The only thing that influences how I would answer that is that it depends on what firehouse you're in. I've seen it. I've seen firehouses where they strictly don't talk to each other. Literally do not talk to each other. And I've seen other firehouses where they're like one big happy family. It always has been this way. It seems to be automatic that the busier firehouses have the best relationships. Whether that's because you have less time to get on each other's nerves or whatever, I don't know. Pride, you know, pride in your company, pride in your job, so on and the ability to not be looking for somebody else to blame for whatever it is. In the old days they had very good camaraderie, too. The difficult period was that maybe five or tens years right after the riots when the influx of the minorities started coming in. For a period of time there was friction which I think has lessened a lot now. I don't know. I'm not on the job now, but I seem to think in a lot of places that's pretty much smoothed over now.

Stoffers: Yes, I'd recommend it. Oh, sure. It's a good job. I mean right now, some of the people you have to work with though. You might not like, but it's still a good job. I enjoyed my career. If I had to do it over again, I'd probably do it again.

McGrory: I enjoyed the job tremendously. I probably didn't want to retire when I retired because I could have stayed on. But I just felt that where I was, I just didn't like what I was seeing. And I didn't think I could be of much help anymore. I just felt as if it was time for me to leave. I didn't want it to be over. You don't want it to be over. It was a lot of good times, but being in headquarters was a different. A lot of fellows who were in the field, they're lucky.

I'd recommend firefighting. Whether I'd recommend the city of Newark? It all depends on the individual. What's going to happen? If you get a good man and he wants to advance? Like I say, I'm not too well versed in the scheme of things when it comes to these exams and everything today. So, you know, what could I tell him? If you don't have a college education and you're going to be working in a factory, certainly the fire department is a lot better. It all depends. It has to be on the individual. I'd have to look at the fellow who was coming on. The last few years that I was on, if you asked me that question, I would have said I wouldn't recommend it. It all depends on what the individual wants.

I think it was better. I don't care who's running the department. I think they can make the department better. Make it better for the guys. As I say, I'm a little lost when it comes to the type of test they have now, whether a man can get advanced. Whether with the roll calls, is it safe enough to put yourself out on a limb as a firefighter, go in that building? Are you going to get the back up or anything? That's what bothers me.

I had so many good times, met so many good people. It was more than just a job going from eight to five or from seven to four or whatever. You had to put up with a lot. You had to give a lot. But you got a lot in return. Why I say that is you go to retirement rackets and you see a lot of men say, "I don't care what anybody says. It's the best job in the world." It is. You have to experience it. You can't explain to anybody. You have to do it. And the more you do of it and the tougher times are maybe that you do it in, the more you enjoy it. That's the way you feel. That's why you get so many guys on the Newark Fire Department feeling that way. That's what draws you all together. That's what makes for you being able to say that the most memorable experience is the whole experience.

Charpentier: I enjoyed the job very much. Would I recommend it today? If they had their heart in it, yes. But just to go for the job, I would hesitate a little. Because the job today is not what it was even ten, fifteen years ago. It's almost an entirely different situation, job, and everything.

Denvir: I loved the job and would certainly recommend it.

Smith: Yes. I did enjoy the job, but I wouldn't recommend it. Now, that seems to be a contradiction. Let me put it this way. I'm not trying to be an elitist or a snob. I would recommend the fire department I started on, not what it is today.

Marcell: I enjoyed it. It was truly a good job, when you work with good guys. I used to like going to fires. I really did. You know the reason why I retired was when I was a young guy it used to take six guys to drag me into the fire building. Now one guy can get me to the second floor. I said, "It was time to get out of this job." (Laughter)

Seriously, we had some good times. I'll tell you nothing was better than come in the firehouse and eat with the guys and stuff. That's really it. You have a good time. You work with all good guys. I'll tell you something. There are not many people in your life who go through this world and have the opportunity that a fireman does because you have the opportunity to save someone's life. You know doctors do that. You don't do that by yourself. A bunch of people do that. When you rescue somebody, there are ten other guys helping you rescue them. You might get the credit, but it takes a team to do everything. It's a life if you look at it. I fooled around an awful lot, but that's how I feel about it. I never worked for a bad chief. I never worked for a bad captain.

Freda: Everyone couldn't wait to go to work. It was fun. There were a lot of fires. Much more work than they have today. There were a lot of fires. There was a lot of camaraderie. There was a lot of fun in the firehouse. Couldn't wait to get out the door of your house some nights to go to work because it was someplace in the world to go and enjoy yourself.

Dunn: I've enjoyed the job immensely. I think as an individual, thinking back over the last thirty-eight years now. From a young kid until the time of becoming a grandfather, it has been the most satisfying and rewarding type of a job you can ever have. I don't think there's anything that can compare with the satisfaction I've had. I don't think there's anything that can compare with the sorrow I've had over the injuries and suffering I've seen people go through. So as far as an emotional funnel, being a fireman is something you can always reflect on and feel good about yourself and the job you've done for the citizens of the city. I would absolutely recommend the job.

Belzer: The job was good to me and I enjoyed it right to the end. I hated to leave it. Lost a lot of good friends too I guess. Over a period of time I didn't see them anymore.

Carragher: Yes, yes. I recommended it to my son. He took the last test two weeks ago. I feel that as much as I don't like what I see going around. I don't like a lot of it. It's still a good job. I think for a guy coming on the job right now. He doesn't know anything that I know about what happened in the past or what was the past. He's here for the future. He may see it go down more than I have. I don't know. But he also may see it come up. As this city turns around, the fire department is going to come up with it. I think when they start doing the buildings over and maybe get new buildings. Get a little more training; we can turn the job around.

Where can you go and get a job today where you're guaranteed a pension in twenty-five years? Or supposing you don't have an education. Say you're the average guy, a high school grad. You want a job. Where can you get a job like this today? I have no reservations at all. My son, I told my son, if he doesn't take the job because he has something else, it doesn't bother me. I'll be happy for him. But if he takes the job, I'll wish him well on the job because he'll do well on the job. But I have no reservations about telling anybody about taking this job, especially if they're qualified. For the right people, I think it's a good job.

Haran: I had my share of fires. I had my good times. Had my bad times, my sad times, heart breaking times, but all in all, I wouldn't trade it for anything. A good job, I met a lot of good men on this job.

Would I recommend it? Absolutely, absolutely, yes, I would recommend the job today. If you want fires, I guess the place around is probably the city of Newark as opposed to the suburbs. It's a good job. The rewards today, financially, are very, very good. There are people with college educations working out there, working hard, not making the money we are. There are guys with no college educations who carry lead ingots in some foundry somewhere making forty grand a year. Don't get me wrong. There are people out there making a hell of a lot more money than we are.

My life is behind me now. My children are grown. My wife is gone. It's more money than I ever need. But I was able to provide a good living. My wife never worked. She raised our children. I always worked part time on this job, but this job always came first. That was always on my mind. This job came first and part time came last. But I always worked part time. I always roofed and put up siding. I had a good part time job. And we always had a good life. We had nice cars. We had nice vacations. My kids had nice clothes. They went to good colleges and it was all because of this job. So this job was good to me. It was very good to me. I have no complaints.

Now, part of it was the fires, the snotty noses, the coming back and talking about it, the sucking a few beers down when you come back from the fire and this and that. I shouldn't say it, but who the hell is going to hear it now. But that was all part of it. That was good. That was all good, the part of going to retirement rackets, the part of going to promotional rackets and meeting the guys. The officers' Christmas parties, this is all part of it. It's all good.

The fires have to be a big part of it also, but we don't get as many fires now. I don't know if I'd tell a guy to go to Bloomfield and be a fireman or go to Nutley and be a fireman or go to West Orange and be a fireman. I'm not sure the camaraderie ever approaches what we had. You have to have the fires.

But yes, I would recommend it. It was a good job to me. I made a good living off of it. I loved it. I loved every minute of it. And I'm getting a good pay for what I'm doing. Years ago I didn't think that. I thought firemen got screwed years ago. I really did. I thought the pay was horse shit.

Butler: I enjoyed the job very much. It's to a point though now, you can say it on the record, I think I've had enough, thirty years and nine months on the job. Today is what? September 3, 1993. October 1, 1993 is my official retirement date. I've enjoyed the work, enjoyed seeing the results of firefighting efforts throughout the years. I made a lot of good friends. Made a few enemies and there's no doubt about it, but nobody's not going to make an enemy. But a lot more friends than enemies and really enjoyed it. That's the one thing. I'm not going to miss the fires, but I am going to miss the guys that I worked with throughout the years. A lot of the close friends I'm still with. Both who have retired before me and who are active on the job. It's my full hope and intention and attention right now to keep in touch with them. Do things because I still have a crowd of guys that I'm friendly with.

We still do things outside the job. Go on a couple of sporting trips and go out to dinner twice a year with our wives so they can continue the relationship they have with each other. And I hope to continue that as long as I'm around anyway.

I would recommend firefighting today, yes, but I would not recommend a young man to come on the job in the city of Newark. I had the occasion in the past year where a young fellow was on a list for the city of Newark. He was also on a list for another city in Hudson County. He came to me because he was in a position where he was number three on the Hudson county list and knew he'd be hired immediately and he was well within range of this first group here. He was in the twenties. He would have been hired now in the city of Newark with this last group. He was a resident of Newark. He came and asked me what I really thought and I sat him down, talked to him for about two hours. Let him talk to some of the younger firemen here. Let him walk out the door. In my opinion he should grab the Hudson county line. I think he was looking that Newark has the reputation around the state as great firefighters. But he took the Hudson county job in a town in Hudson County.

Came back to me about two months ago, sat and spent two hours with me thanking me for pushing him to there. Because he says it's a great department. He believes that it's a lot better organized, a lot better run and they got a contract now that almost stays right with the city of Newark. Dollar wise he's not losing much. It's a smaller department. I think he's going to be a lot happier. But the fire service in general, I'd recommend it to anybody.

Cahill: I absolutely enjoyed the job. The only reservation I have to recommending it to one of my sons for example today, at least in this city, would be the affirmative action. I don't think there's much room here for them to advance like we could have. When I talk about the Maplewood or Morristown Fire Departments, I'd say yes.

Highsmith: I've enjoyed every phase of the job. Like I said, when I was sitting on that corner on Frelinghuysen Avenue and Fenwick Street, I was getting tired of fighting fires. That's when I left the firefighting. I went over to Fire Prevention. I enjoyed that for ten years. I enjoyed the camaraderie. I enjoyed the leadership. I enjoyed the hours. I enjoyed my holidays and Saturdays and Sundays off and nights off. I really enjoyed that. When the paperwork got high, I didn't enjoy that anymore; went to the Arson Squad. I worked there. I worked tours. I couldn't stand working nights. I hated nights. I started working days. Then I had to go back to nights because of manpower shortages. I came to work every night, but I disliked it.

I was getting stressed out. We have a scanner in the office. Every time the joker would hit, I'd jump sky high. I had to sleep by the telephone. Guys in the field don't understand. They might see me out once a night in the Arson Squad, but they don't know. I've been up all night answering phones, filling out complaints. And it was getting to me. It was stressing me out. I thought that I had used up all my usefulness in the fire department. I enjoyed every bit of it, but I knew it was time for me to go because I was letting it worry me and it's not supposed to worry me. Anytime anything that's enjoyable to you becomes a hassle to you, it's time to leave.

I left not because of guys I worked with because they were all beautiful. I had beautiful partners that I worked with, beautiful guys, beautiful Captains, and Chief Raymond, prince of a chief, but the job itself.

I was relegated to doing the book? That's what I was doing. I was even worried about that. When I came in the morning, I was worried about keeping the book straight. I was worried about the guys who were working. Not filling out you trip sheet, not having all their jobs done.

I would listen to their jobs. I would try and give input in their jobs. Not to pick a personal one. Each tour's job, I'm trying to give them input. I try to play the devil's advocate. Suppose this suppose that, well that guy's not wrong. It started getting to me. I started becoming more involved towards the end of my career than I was when I was just working my tours, because I just had a partner and had to be worried about what I was doing. Now I'm worried about what everybody's doing. It was getting to be too much.

Then I just sat back and I said, "I really don't need the stress and strain." I have done all I can, that I think that I can do. Just staying any longer would be just collecting a paycheck. Because after it gets on me, I'd just be coming to work and saying the hell with everything. Just stay for my eight hours and go home. But I didn't want it to end like that. I ended on a high note within me and that's why I thought it was time to get out. That's just why I left.

I would recommend this job to anybody. As a matter of fact, guys on the job now will tell you, "Rock's the one who got me the job. He's responsible for me getting the job." See I gave out applications to many guys.

Cody: Oh, I definitely enjoyed the job. Except for that short period, but that was so small. Even though I consider that the dark part of my career; it was still great. It was still great because I was at Six Engine and I was doing what I like to do. I enjoyed fighting fires, without a doubt. We didn't get rich. You enjoyed doing what you're doing.

Would I recommend the job? Definitely, even as bad as people say it is now, I would still say it beats plenty of jobs. It doesn't beat a lot of jobs. I mean if I was on Wall Street making like a couple million dollars or something that's different. If you're going to drive a bus or if you're going to be a mailman or a cop, why wouldn't you come here? Be this, be a fireman. It's good. It's a good job. But again, you have to be with the right people.

Garrity: I loved it. You know you're like the peg, the square peg that fits in the square hole. I fit. From the day I walked in, I fit. It didn't take me ten minutes to find my little niche and sit in it. I never regret any of it.

I would absolutely recommend it. As a matter of fact, I saw a kid in City Hall who got laid off. He took the test. He passed the written. He passed the physical. I was just talking to him yesterday and he wants to go on the job. A couple of guys said, "Ah, it's a shitty job." It's not a shitty job. It's not. I was talking to Jack Maloney a couple of weeks ago. He says, "Who would have thought when you were a baggy ass fireman walking in the front door you'd end up here?" Look what the fire department did for me. I went in with a high school education, hated school and eventually got talked into going to school. I ended up with a job like this, plus the pension. Not too many of us are going to starve.

That wasn't what I went to the fire department for. I wasn't looking for retiring. Twenty-two years old, retiring? That's so far down the road you're not even thinking about it. In fact then you had to have twenty-five years of service and be fifty-five years of age. I'm not fifty-five yet and I'm out almost two years. I'll be out two years next month. The job is fantastic.

You have to work with the right people. A lot of times that means you have to move around until you find the right people. The only thing is, it's much slower. And I think it's going to continue to stay slow. They're not going to have the work that we had in the '60s, '70s, and early '80s. They're not going to have that.

But other than that if you can find a good crew to work with, who enjoy the work. Not guys that have to get out to go PT or having four or five guys working for them so you don't see them for a week at a time. The guys who enjoy the fire department want to work in it. It's a good job. I couldn't have had a better job. I mean, what the hell, they made me a chief for nothing. They don't do that every place. They'll probably never do it again. I left as Battalion Chief, second step Battalion Chief, with a high school education.

All the bad nights, all the good nights, I don't remember the bad nights. I remember the real funny nights just sitting around the firehouse having a good time laughing and giggling. The times like when Mike Moran got killed. That was a real bad night for us. That's the only night I worked where a firefighter was killed in the line of duty. I never worked any other night. I remember that, but I remember more the better times than I remember the things like that.

When I got up to Avon Avenue, both those companies really liked what they were doing and enjoyed it. That's why I stayed, because they really liked the work. As dirty, shitty, scary, dangerous as it was at times, they enjoyed it. They had a lot of fun doing it and that's what the job is all about. If you're not having fun, you shouldn't be doing it.

Wargo: Yes, I did enjoy the job, especially when I was in the firehouse. Before I got promoted, I had good friends when I worked in Eight Truck.

Guys in Sixteen Engine, Eight Engine, we worked really well together. Some of them I came on the job with. Then when I went to One Engine, I made friends. I liked it. I enjoyed it. I enjoyed the changes in working in one place to another. But after you get sick and you can't do the firefighting anymore, the ecstasy starts to wear a little bit. It becomes a job.

Yes, I probably would recommend the job to my son. It's still a good job. Like I said, hopefully Newark will never see the civil disorders that we saw in the last twenty-five years. The pay is pretty good and the apparatus are better.

McGovern: Yes, I still enjoy it. I don't enjoy it as much as I used to, but I still enjoy it. It's easier to enjoy as a fireman. You have no responsibility as a fireman. You could sit back and do what you want. But I enjoyed it as a Captain. I enjoyed it more as a Captain, than I do as a Chief, but you can't look back. You have to look ahead. How can I make it more enjoyable? That's all.

I'd recommend it to anybody. I don't know if I want my son to be a fireman. I never thought about it, but he doesn't want to be fireman. If he did, I don't think I'd want him to. If he could make a living another way and enjoy doing it, I'd rather he did that. I wouldn't seek him to be a legacy. You could die on this job. It's as simple as that. It's very easy. If you could make the same money and have as much enjoyment in another career, why buy into the risk. Other than that, I'd recommend it for anybody else's son.

Prachar: I loved this job. I said that from the beginning. I've gotten myself into a couple of jams in the past year or so, where I hated this job. Hopefully I just got myself back into the situation where I can't wait to get to the job. It meant nothing to me before I got promoted, to come to work three-thirty in the afternoon to relieve a guy because I loved the job. In the last five months or so I couldn't care less about he job. Hopefully that was my down part of my rollercoaster. Maybe I'll come back up for my last couple of years because I could go within twenty-four months.

Finucan: I love this job. I'd recommend this job to anybody. It's a good job. You have to know what you're getting into too. The dangerous job is still there. It's got a lot of problems. Still if you're an ambitious person and you're looking for the promotional end of it, there's a risk factor there that you're going to have to accept. I would recommend it. If I had a son, it would depend on the kid's nature. I'm of the opinion that each person is an individual and you try to steer them in one direction and just help them to grow. If the kid was not interested in being a doctor or a lawyer or some sort of a professional or an airline pilot or something like that and he was just kind of looking around for something to do, I wouldn't hesitate to recommend the fire department. I would hope that he would get his education first, but if he said that the fire department was what he wanted to do then I would say fine. It's a good job for me and I like the job.

When I look back on it and I look at my friends who are in other fields, I have to say that although I may not have made the money that they make, mine was the better career. I did all of the things that I wanted to do along the way. You have to see the trees through the woods. You have to enjoy a little as you go along and the fire department absolutely lets you do that. You have the time. It's no high stress. At least I never took the job home with me. When you leave here or when I left here there wasn't a mound of paper work that I had to worry about. When I went out on vacation and I think everybody on the job knows you go out on vacation, you come back, it's like nobody missed you. You come back and you just fall back in step and you're there again. For all those reasons, it's not a bad job, if that's what you're looking for.

Rotunda: I love the job. Before I lay down every time I look up in the air and I say, "I love this job." I'm not kidding about that. Honestly, where do you get the relaxation, being with the guys, and the excitement? People even like you when it comes down to it because they call you for everything. They call you for sickness. They call you for electricity. They call you for broken pipes. Sometimes they call us for fires also. But seriously, I think it's the best thing I did. Lost a lot of money doing it, but as far as life goes, I've enjoyed it.

McDonnell: Yes, I still would recommend the job. I wish there was hope for the department because then it could become a good department again. You need to make several changes. You need to go back to what you had, to what worked. You need to go back to a legitimate civil service system. You need somebody at the top who cares and is willing to instill some discipline. You've gone downhill. When you try to institute these things they're going to be fought tooth and nail, but you need somebody who's going to say fuck you. You can bitch and moan all you want, but this is the way it's going to be. I think that guys will eventually, they'll get over it. They resist it at first, but they'll find it's not all that hard. That's why I wish that would happen. Hopefully it will happen. They have to get a change of leadership.

Without some kind of change in the civil service testing, coming on the job and going through the ranks, nothing is going to. If you don't have knowledge, you have the blind leading the blind. You need competent people. The way you have it now you get incompetent people getting promoted to positions of authority where whoever comes into their command is going to be just as incompetent as they are. Hopefully, people wise up and get back to that. It was a shame that they did away with civil service's merit system because it really served people well in this country. It was, no matter what they say, it was a legitimate attempt to get a competent person. It had nothing to do with his race.

T. Grehl: I tried to get my son to take it. So the answer is yes, I would recommend it. I would because these were the best memories I've ever had. I enjoyed it immensely, immensely and especially the time with those guys on Springfield Avenue.

Carter: Because I enjoyed my job so much, I didn't study and I didn't make Battalion Chief years ahead of where I should have, because I was an asshole and made the mistake of loving my job.

Would I recommend the job to my son? If you're going to frame it as the traditional parent's aspiration for a child, I just want my kid to be happy at what he does. I will support him whichever way he way seeks to go, but I will not guide him in any particular direction. If he asks for advice, I'd say, if you can handle certain people and you can put up with getting dumped on, but then you want to achieve something, and you want to handle severe frustrations, perhaps you should consider this as a job. The point being, I would not actively solicit him to be a career fireman, but I would gladly welcome him into the ranks of the volunteers at home with me because of the different environment.

You can't get around the racial issue which is ruining things on the Newark Fire Department. That's it. If you can learn to live with that and accept that as a given and work to find all of the good that still exists in the Newark Fire Department, then this job can be very good. But you have to actively do this. In the old days you used to walk down the street and it would fall out of a door and hit you. Now you have to work at it.

Langenbach: It's still a great job. I would use caution. My son wants to be a fireman and I always tell him the good and the bad. It's not the way it was. You can't listen to my stories from 1976 and think you're going to walk into a firehouse and find that because those days are over. We're never going to have the fires we had back then. Thank God. So, you're not going to do that. It's still a great life I think. Anybody who knocks this job is out of their mind. I put two kids through college on this job, got a nice house, and took care of my family. Yes, I'd still recommend the job; just have to come in with open eyes. You can't come in here and expect that it's going to be Backdraft.

I enjoyed the job, absolutely, absolutely. Yes, like I said in the beginning, in being a fireman on Belmont Avenue was probably the greatest experience I ever had.

Connell: I loved it, until they put me on straight days. Straight days, it's not the same. Would I recommend it? As much as I say no, yes. I keep on saying you got to be nuts. I feel sorry for anybody coming on this job. But between you and me, if I had it all over again, I wish I could be just coming on the job, start all over again.

Langevin: I've enjoyed virtually every day, every day that I've been on the fire department, but I wouldn't recommend the job today. You can come on this job now when you're eighteen. I would rather see somebody get an education or get some military experience first and then possibly take the job. I came on the job when I was twenty-five and I didn't go to college or anything. I had my military experience, but to an eighteen year old, I would not recommend it. Like I said, I would recommend college, if you can do college or a stint in the military and then try it. After that I would recommend it. I mean, if this is your calling, if this is what you really want to do, then go for it. But get a little life experience first or some education.

Perdon: Absolutely enjoyed the job. I didn't take the chief's test. I like what I'm doing now. You still like being in the shit. Yes, I do. Yes, I do. I mean it's too slow for me right now. I couldn't handle Six Engine again, not at my age. But I still enjoy, big time going to fires, putting out, doing as best you can.

I miss not being with the people I was with though. I'm talking about going back into all the people I was around, all the other companies. That's one thing I can't impress on these newer guys enough. Just the surrounding companies, they were good. Everybody was good. You always thought you were better. You don't go and say you were the best, but you were second to none. You know what I mean? There's nobody better. Let me put it to you that way. There're a lot of equals, but definitely nobody better.

Bisogna: Yes, I enjoyed it. I have no complaints. I liked this job from walking in the door. Don't get me wrong. It's had its moments. I've have some disagreements with some guys, with a captain at one time. We ironed it out. At the time that it happened, it wasn't the most fun thing because I was coming to work going "I don't want to go to work. I don't know what's going to happen today." Not that I was a bad guy or anything, it's just that we had a personality conflict for a couple of months. I think he was nuts, but hey maybe I was nuts. That was the only time I was on my way to work going "Ah, Geeze. What's going to go on today?"

But other than that, it's been great. I mean how many guys look forward to going to work no matter what happens? You go in expecting to read the paper, have a cup of coffee, put yourself on the rig and read a book or whatever. Do some inspections and if you got fires, all the more fun. Where else do they tell you to break windows and cut holes and get dirty and laugh about it, very carefree type of job. I always said, "If you got a fire and we show up, how bad can we do?" I mean if we're to yell, "Look out" when the building falls down, at least somebody came to yell look out. It's not like it's a job where "Hey, you only made two airplanes today. We expected four." You're going there to TRY to protect lives and property. It's not written in stone it's going to happen. I mean you may get there a minute too late or you might make a nice save. You don't know. But, no I have no regrets. I would do it again.

Yes, I would recommend it. I would. I think it's a fulfilling job for somebody. The only down part of it is, sometimes I'll go home and my wife will ask, "What's the matter?" I say, "It's firehouse blues." You're here two days. You don't do hardily anything, especially these days in this company it's not that busy. This is maybe one step above the Burg really. It's a well-kept secret over here. You get home and you go like well what did I do today? I have nothing to show. There's no production. So you try to keep yourself busy. Maybe if you're an "A" type personality where you have to have that constant feedback, this might not be the job for you. Maybe that's why there's divorce and depression and things like that attached to this job. You've got to guard against that I think. And the longer you're on the job, the worse that gets too. You get older and you start to think back and you wonder, "Well, what am I doing? What am I contributing?" There is that void that this job provides. When you're busy, there's no problem, as long as you do something.

Ricca: Yes, I enjoy the job. I always felt I'm going to have to be carried out of here in a box. I'd recommend it to anybody. To my son, if it were twenty years ago, yes. Not today though because of the fact that the way things are even though you study, it doesn't mean you're going to advance. But had it been twenty years ago, yes, I'd recommend it, maybe even fifteen years ago. Now no, except to the person who was undecided who didn't want to go to college.

Gesualdo: Oh, yes, I'm happy. I still love coming to work. Get up, don't ever have a hesitation to come into work, unless there's three feet of snow on the ground. I'd seriously think about calling in on sick leave. The way it's been it seems over the last five years or so, we always seem to be at work when it snows. I don't have that issue to deal with too much, but no it's still a lot of fun coming in. I never look back.

But I wouldn't recommend it to my son. The reason being because it's too limited, it's too limiting. You have your promotions obviously, but I think when you're in civil service you're limited in your ability to do something, mainly because of the shift work and working nights. I like to think of the career as a job, have a little more flexibility, a little more movement. That's the only thing I find about the fire department. Once you're in it, you're kind of locked into it. A lot of guys have other careers and other businesses, but I think those are the individuals who aren't really great firefighters. They're more involved in their other businesses. To be a good firefighter, I think it has to be your primary concern.

List of Interviewees

Baldino, Captain Barney, letter to the author 20 September, 2002. (appointed 1951)

Belzger, Firefighter William, 4 October, 2004, transcript. (appointed 1959)

Bisogna, Captain Joseph, 25 July, 2001, transcript. (appointed 1974)

Butler, Captain James, 3 September 1993, transcript. (appointed 1963)

Cahill, Firefighter Joseph, 25 June 1991, transcript. (appointed 1963)

Carragher, Deputy Chief William, November 1994, transcript. (appointed 1960)

Carter, Battalion Chief Harry, 12 June, 1991, transcript. (appointed 1973)

Charpentier, Firefighter Frederick, 22 August 1993, transcript. (appointed 1959)

Cody, Battalion Chief James, 26 October 1999, transcript. (appointed 1964)

Connell, Battalion Chief Anthony, 26 February, 1999, 24 November, 2003. (appointed 1974)

Cosby, Firefighter Joseph, 22 August, 1991, transcript. (appointed 1969)

Denvir, Captain John, 13 September 1993, transcript. (appointed 1959)

Deutch, Firefighter Charles, 14 November 1993, transcript. (appointed 1953)

Dunn, Deputy Chief Edward, 14 August1991, 29 August 1997, transcript. (appointed 1959)

Finucan, Deputy Chief James, 7 August 1991, transcript. (appointed 1969)

Freda, Deputy Chief Alfred, 12, 25, 26 July 1991, transcript. (appointed 1959)

Fredette, Firefighter Reggie, 3 November, 1993, transcript. (appointed 1942)

Freeman, Captain Richard, 20, 21 August 1991, transcript. (appointed 1956)

Garrity, Battalion Chief Joseph, May 1992, transcript. (appointed 1964)

Gesualdo, Captain Al, 21 July, 2003, transcript. (appointed 1978)

Grehl, Deputy Chief Frederick, 7 August 1993, transcript. (appointed 1948)

Grehl, Captain Thomas, 29 May, 2002, transcript. (appointed 1971)

Griffith, Chief Fire Alarm Operator Robert, 3 July, 1991, transcript. (appointed 1953)

Haran, Captain Edward, 5 February 2001, transcript. (appointed 1961)

Harris, Captain William, 13 December 1999, transcript. (appointed 1961)

Highsmith, Firefighter Gerald, 2 June 1994, transcript. (appointed 1963)

Kinnear, Deputy Chief David, 28 September 1992, transcript. (appointed 1947)

Knight, Firefighter Gerald, 19 June 1991, transcript. (appointed 1964)

Langenbach, Deputy Chief James, 24 October, 2002, transcript. (appointed 1973)

Langevin, Firefighter Robert, 23 February, 1999, transcript. (appointed 1974)

Luxton, Captain Charles, 14 January, 1999, transcript. (appointed 1973)

Marcell, Firefighter Andrew, 23 September 1998, transcript. (appointed 1959)

Masters, Firefighter Anthony, 24 March, 2004, transcript. (appointed 1947)

Masterson, Captain Andrew, 6 April, 2005, transcript. (appointed 1949)

McCormack, Sr. Deputy Chief James, 14 June 1991, transcript. (appointed 1949)

McDonnell, Captain Thomas, 30 March, 1999, 16 April, 1999, transcript. (appointed 1970)

McGee, Captain Raymond, 26 October 2000, transcript. (appointed 1956)

McGovern, Battalion Chief Thomas, 8 June, 2001, transcript. (appointed 1968)

McGrory. Deputy Chief Albert, 31 August 1991, transcript. (appointed 1957)

Melodick, Firefighter William, June, 2001, transcript. (appointed 1970)

Miller, Battalion Chief Joseph, 16, 21 August 1991, transcript. (appointed 1959)

Perdon, Captain George, 9 June, 2003, transcript. (appointed 1974)

Pianka, Firefighter George, 15 June, 2001, transcript. (appointed 1970)

Pignato, Captain Nicholas, 26 May, 1999, transcript. (appointed 1974)

Prachar, Captain Daniel, 12 August, 1991, transcript. (appointed 1968)

Redden, Fire Chief Joseph, 16 September 2002, transcript. (appointed 1947)

Ricca, Battalion Chief Ronald, 1 June, 2000, transcript. (appointed 1974)

Rotonda, Firefighter Gerard, 3 May, 2000, transcript. (appointed 1970)

Ryan, Battalion Chief Joseph, 28 September, 1999, transcript. (appointed 1973)

Smith, Firefighter James, 2 September 1998, transcript. (appointed 1959)

Stoffers, Battalion Chief Carl, 2 September 1998, transcript. (appointed 1956)

Vesey, Firefighter Edward, 15 June 1999, transcript. (appointed 1948)

Vetrini, Captain Joseph, 14 September, 1993, transcript. (appointed 1946)

Wall, Deputy Chief Edward, 13 September, 2000, transcript. (appointed 1954)

Wargo, Captain Andrew, 6 June 1991, transcript. (appointed 1964)

www.ingramcontent.com/pod-product-compliance
Lightning Source LLC
Chambersburg PA
CBHW021052090426
42738CB00006B/297